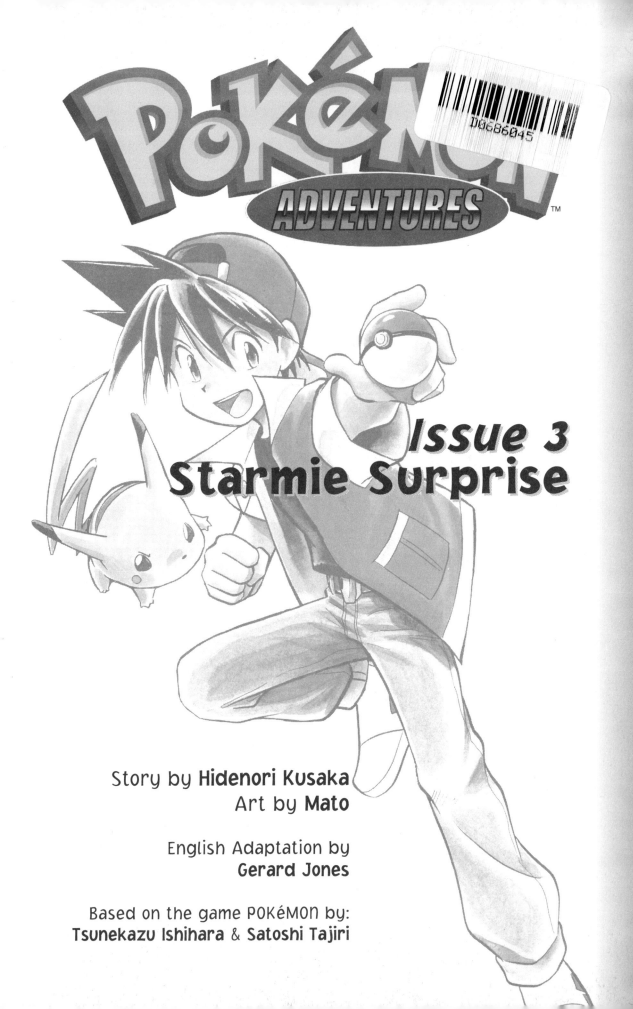

POKéMON ADVENTURES ™

Issue 3
Starmie Surprise

Story by **Hidenori Kusaka**
Art by **Mato**

English Adaptation by
Gerard Jones

Based on the game POKéMON by:
Tsunekazu Ishihara & **Satoshi Tajiri**

POKéMON ADVENTURES
Issue 3:
Starmie Surprise

Story/Hidenori Kusaka
Art/Mato

English Adaptation/Gerard Jones

Translation/Kaori Inoue
Touch-up & Lettering/Dan Nakrosis
Graphics & Design/Carolina Ugalde
Editing/William Flanagan

Editor-in-Chief/Hyoe Narita
Publisher/Seiji Horibuchi

First published by
Shogakukan, Inc. in Japan.

Published by Viz Comics
P.O. Box 77064
San Francisco, CA 94107

For advertising opportunities, call:
Oliver Chin
Director of Sales and Marketing
(415) 546-7073 ext. 128

Ask for our **free**
Viz Shop-By-Mail catalog!

Call toll free: (800) 394-3042
Or visit us on-line at our web site:
www.viz.com. And check out our
internet magazines: j-pop.com at
www.j-pop.com and Animerica at
www.animerica-mag.com! Get your
free Viz newsletter at j-pop.com!

CONTENTS

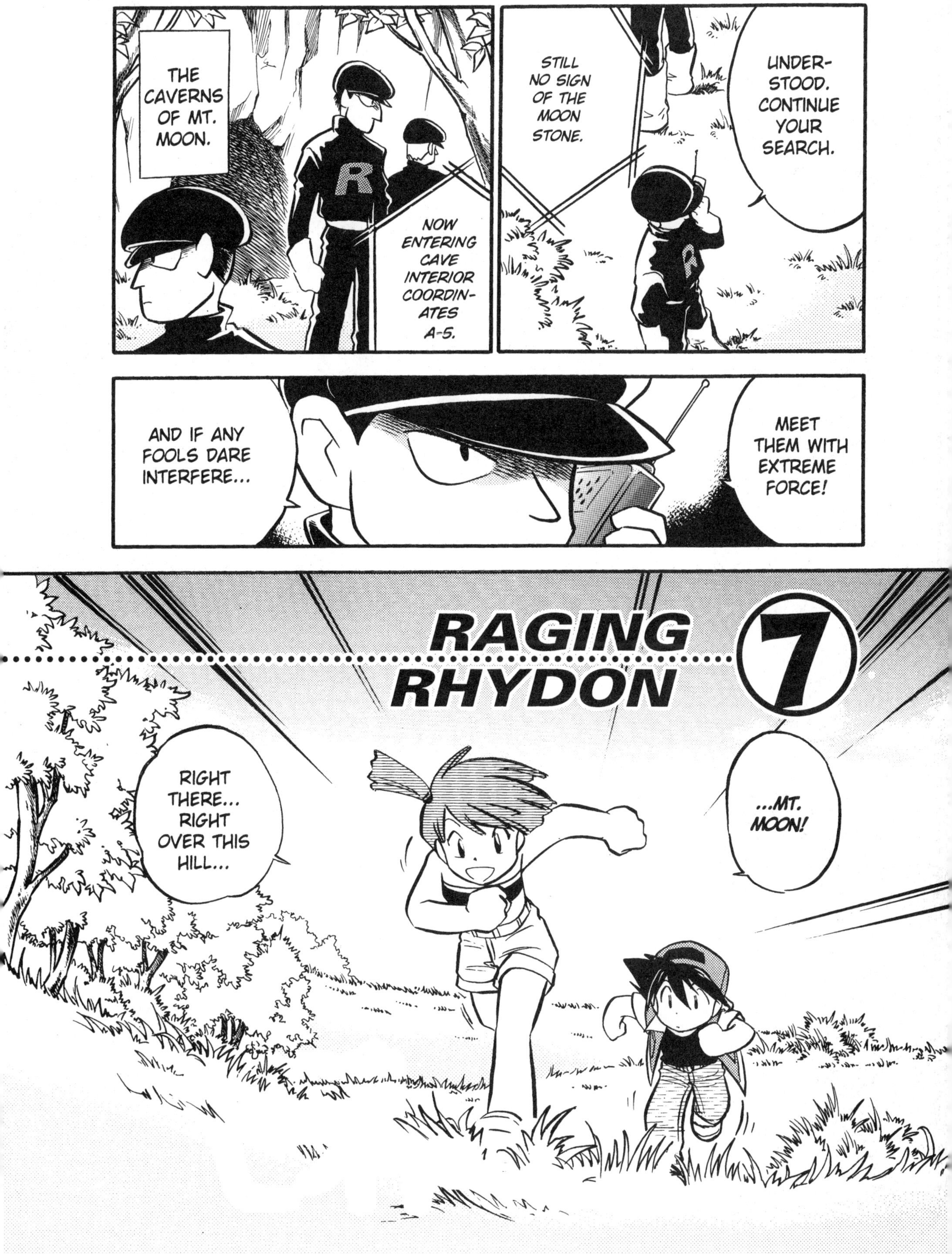
THE CAVERNS OF MT. MOON.
NOW ENTERING CAVE INTERIOR COORDINATES A-5.
STILL NO SIGN OF THE MOON STONE.
UNDERSTOOD. CONTINUE YOUR SEARCH.
AND IF ANY FOOLS DARE INTERFERE...
MEET THEM WITH EXTREME FORCE!
RAGING RHYDON
7
RIGHT THERE... RIGHT OVER THIS HILL...
...MT. MOON!

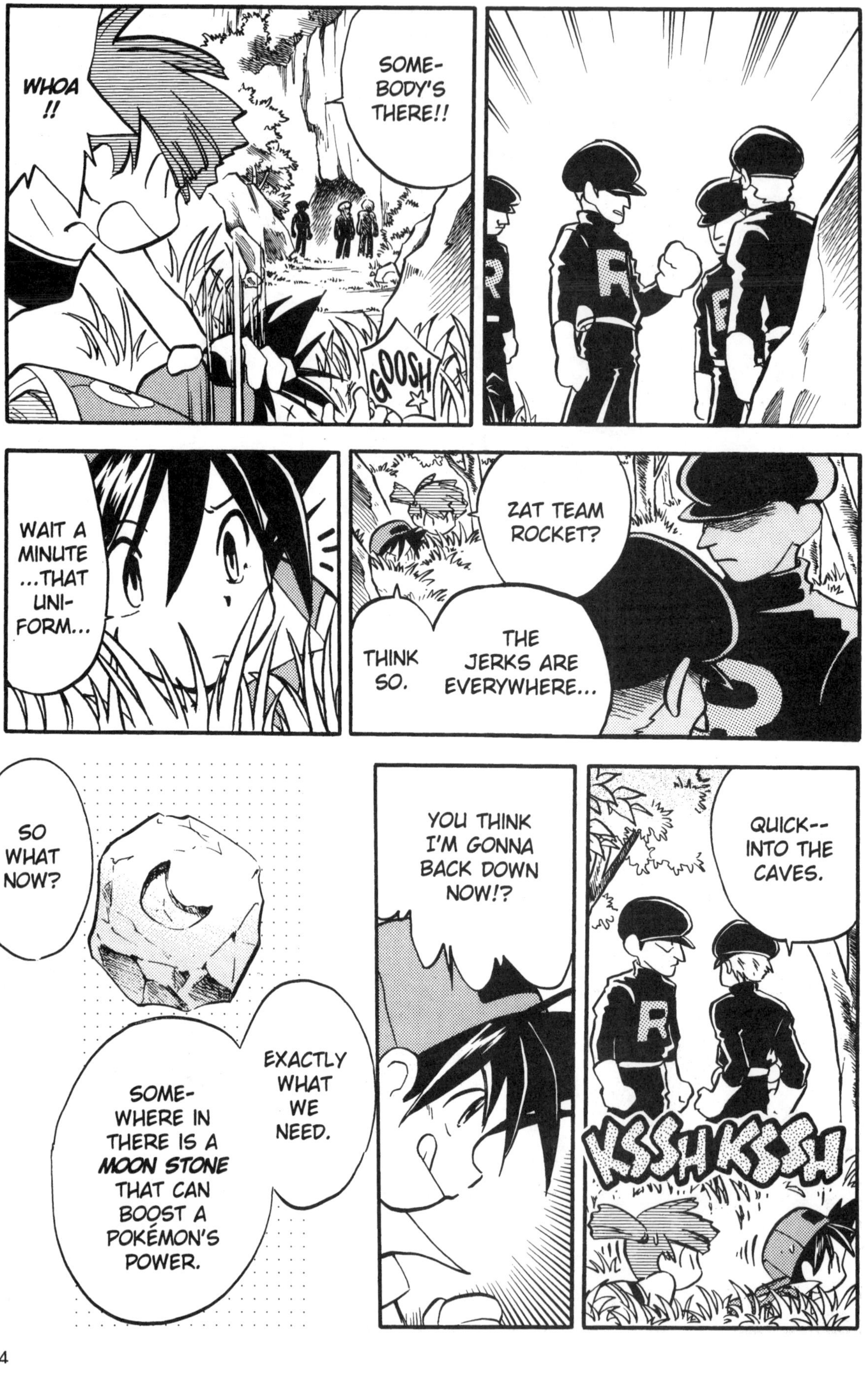
WHOA !!
SOME-BODY'S THERE!!
GOOSH
WAIT A MINUTE ...THAT UNI-FORM...
ZAT TEAM ROCKET?
THINK SO.
THE JERKS ARE EVERYWHERE...
SO WHAT NOW?
SOME-WHERE IN THERE IS A **MOON STONE** THAT CAN BOOST A POKÉMON'S POWER.
EXACTLY WHAT WE NEED.
YOU THINK I'M GONNA BACK DOWN NOW!?
QUICK--INTO THE CAVES.
KSSH KSSH

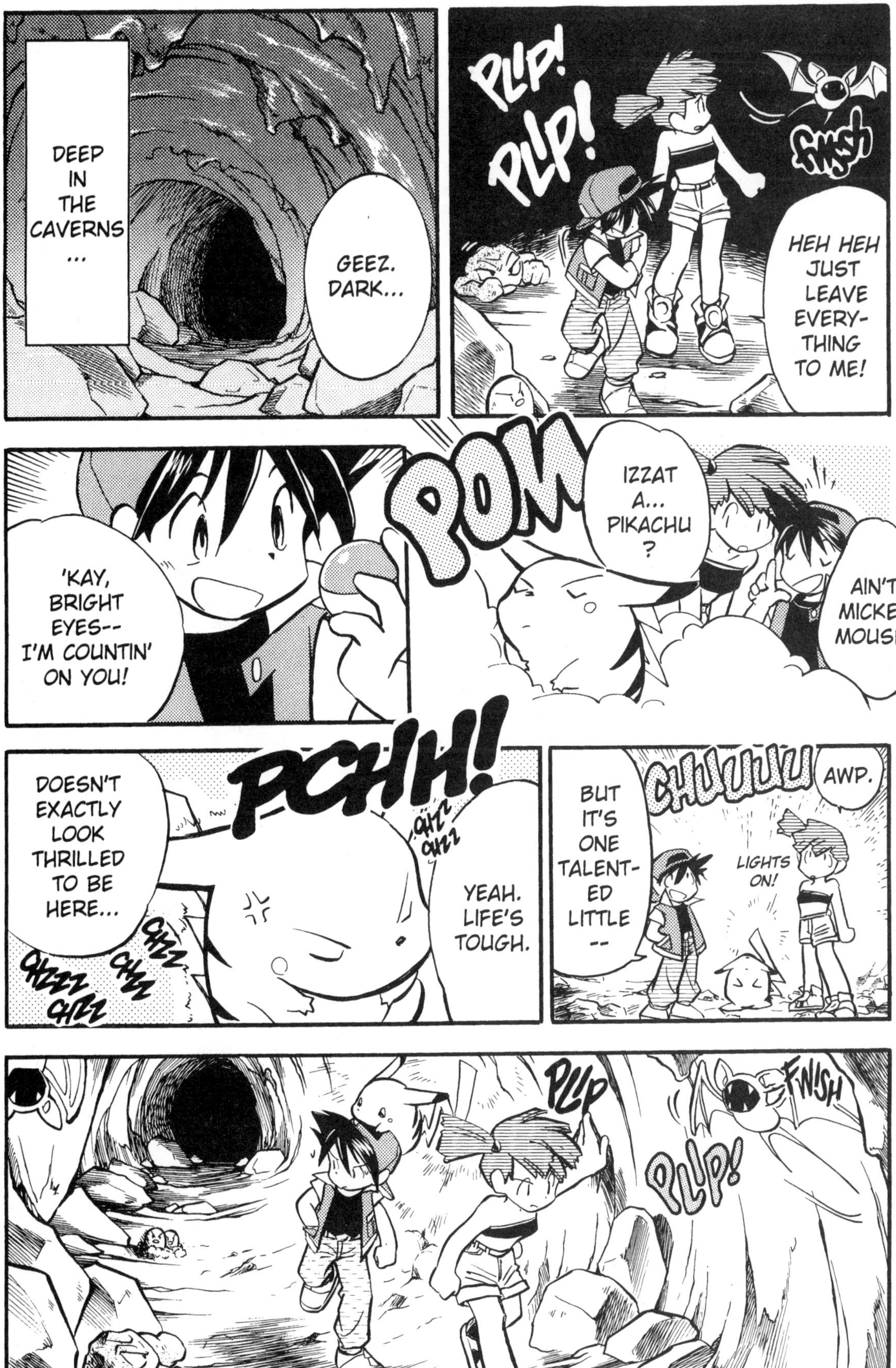
DEEP IN THE CAVERNS ...
GEEZ. DARK...
PLIP! PLIP!
FWISH
HEH HEH JUST LEAVE EVERY-THING TO ME!
'KAY, BRIGHT EYES-- I'M COUNTIN' ON YOU!
POM
IZZAT A... PIKACHU ?
AIN'T MICKEY MOUSE.
PCHH!
DOESN'T EXACTLY LOOK THRILLED TO BE HERE...
CHZZ CHZZ
CHZZ CHZZ CHZZZ CHZZ
YEAH. LIFE'S TOUGH.
CHUUUU
AWP.
BUT IT'S ONE TALENT-ED LITTLE --
LIGHTS ON!
PLIP
FWISH
PLIP!

YUURRG!!

STUPID ROCK, I OUGHTTA...

RED... LOOK UP...

HUH?

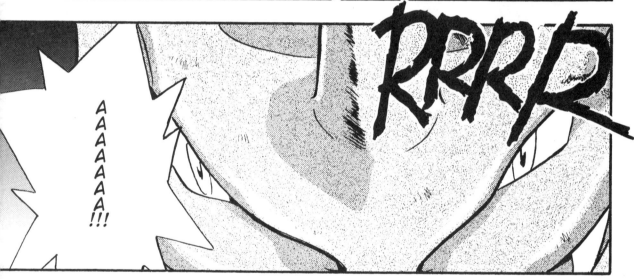

AAAAAAA!!!

RRRR

HEH!

WELL. IF IT ISN'T TOM SAWYER AND LITTLE BECKY IN THE CAVE.

POP!

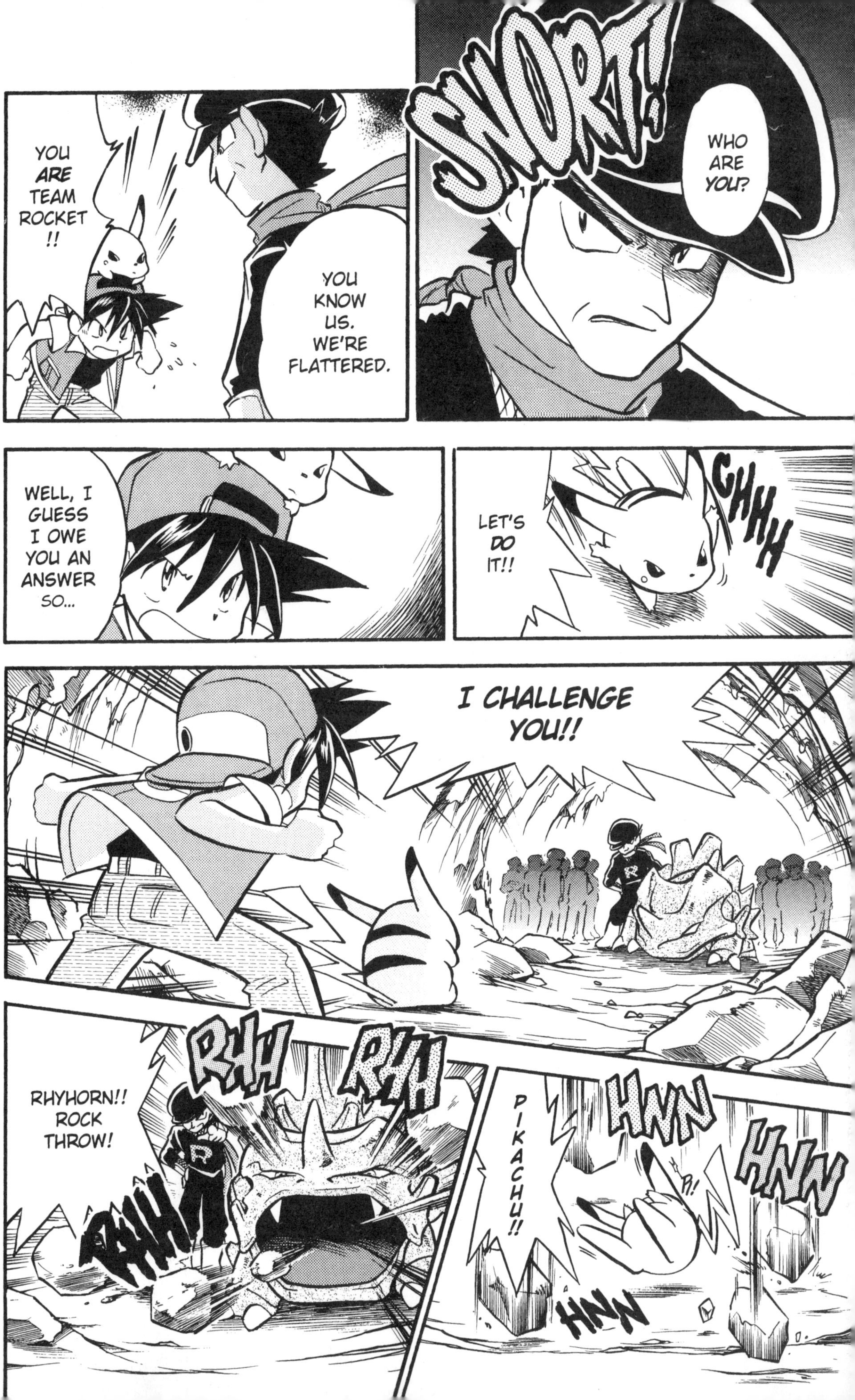
SNORT!
WHO ARE YOU?
YOU ARE TEAM ROCKET!!
YOU KNOW US. WE'RE FLATTERED.
CHHHH
LET'S DO IT!!
WELL, I GUESS I OWE YOU AN ANSWER SO...
I CHALLENGE YOU!!
HNN
HNN
PIKACHU!!
HNN
RYH
RYH
RHYHORN!! ROCK THROW!
RYHH

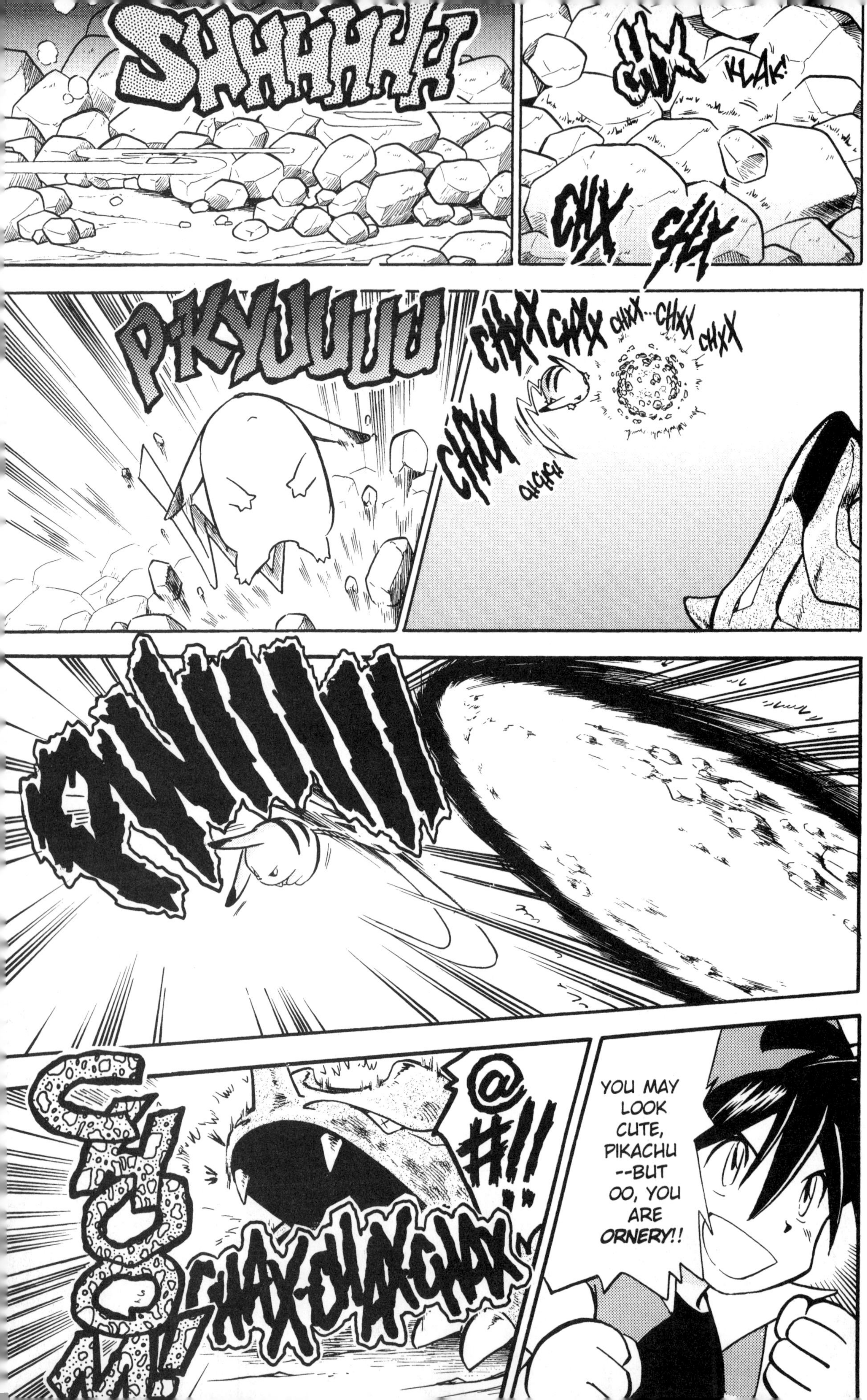
KLAK!
CHX
SHX
P-KYUUUUU
CHXX CHXX CHXX CHXX...CHXX CHXX
CHXX
@#!!
CHAX-CHAX-CHAX
YOU MAY LOOK CUTE, PIKACHU --BUT OO, YOU ARE ORNERY!!

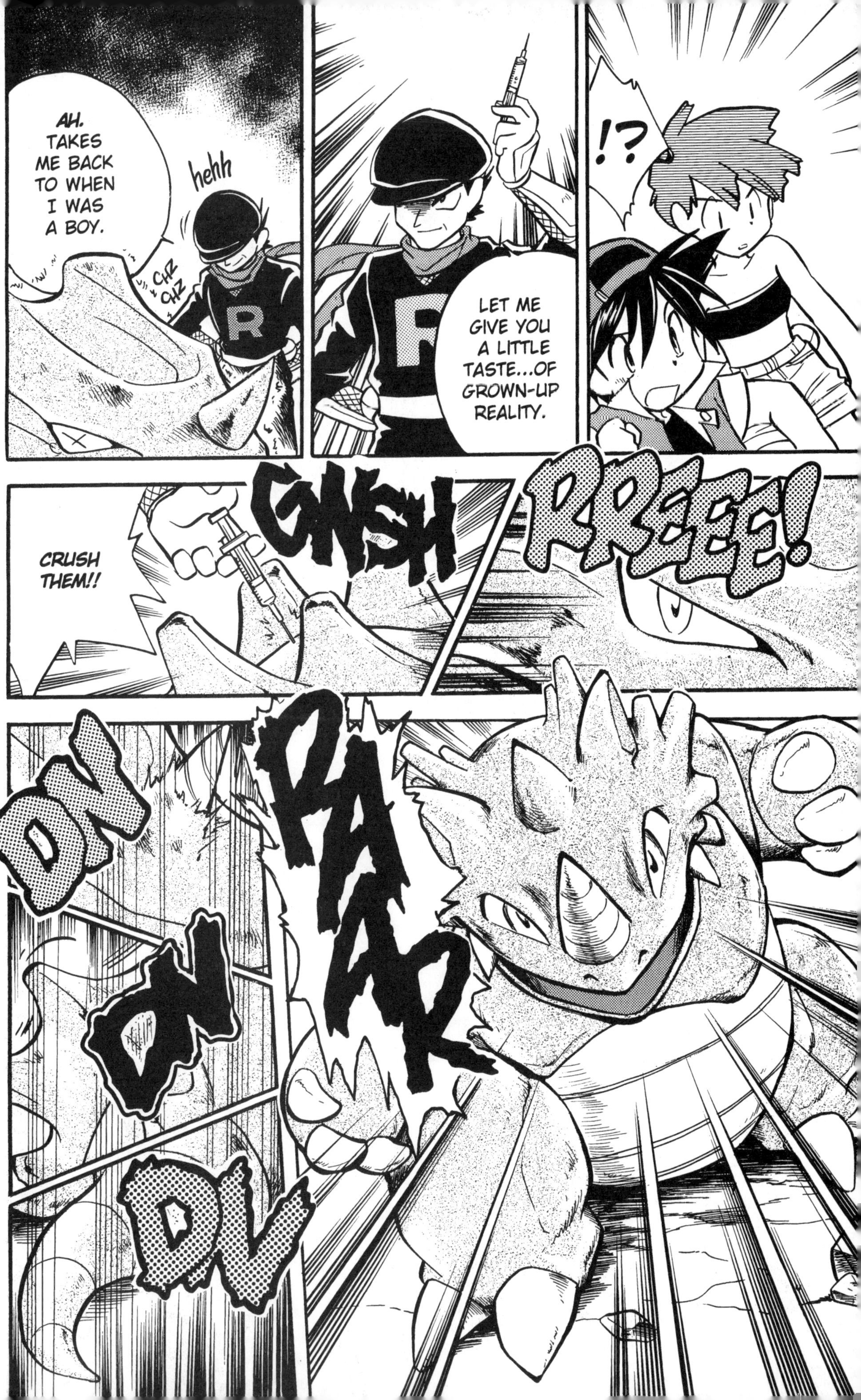
AH. TAKES ME BACK TO WHEN I WAS A BOY.
hehh
CHZ CHZ
LET ME GIVE YOU A LITTLE TASTE...OF GROWN-UP REALITY.
!?
CRUSH THEM!!
GNSH
RREEE!
DN
DN
DN
PAAR

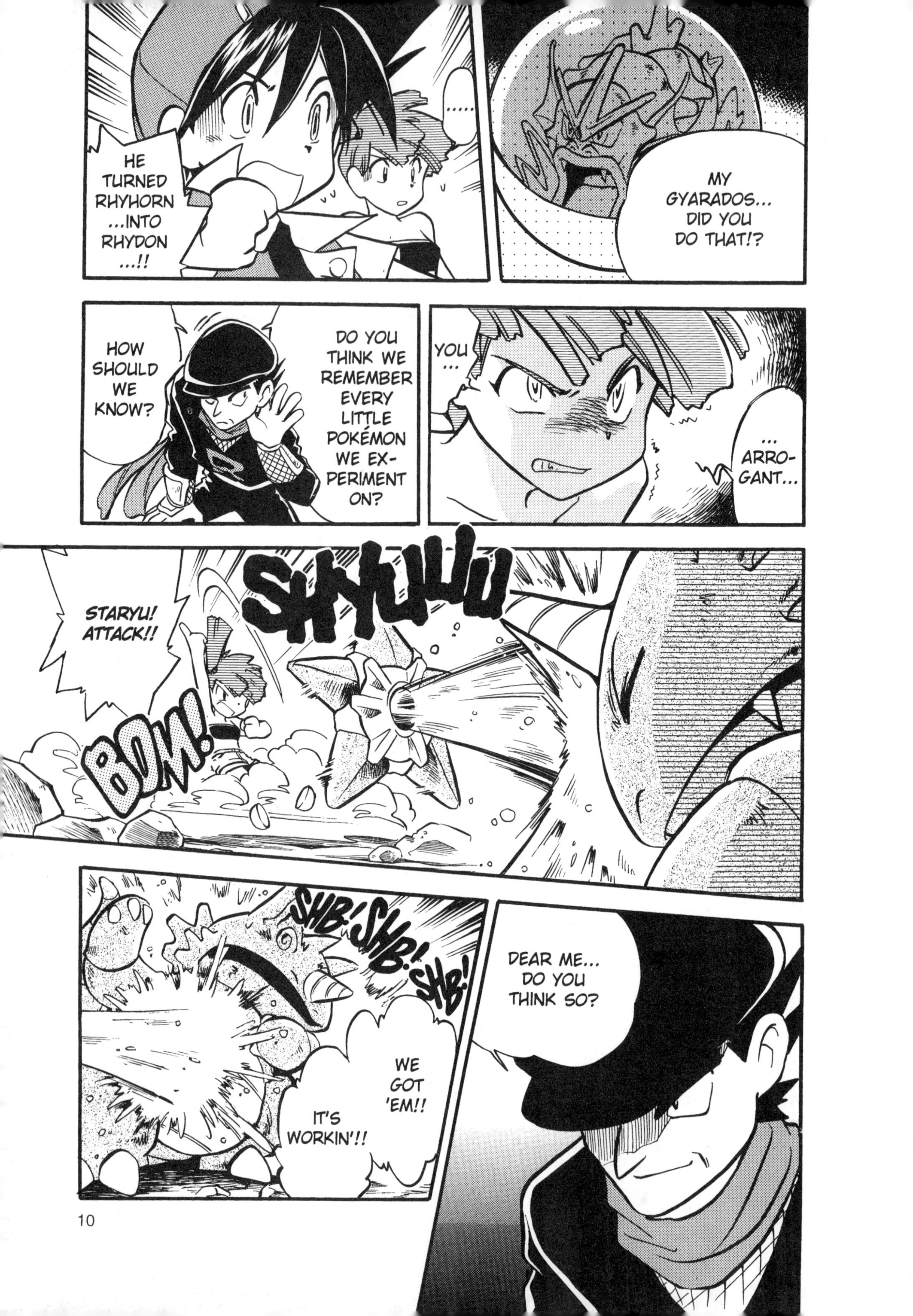

MY GYARADOS... DID YOU DO THAT!?
......
HE TURNED RHYHORN ...INTO RHYDON ...!!
YOU ...
... ARRO-GANT...
DO YOU THINK WE REMEMBER EVERY LITTLE POKÉMON WE EX-PERIMENT ON?
HOW SHOULD WE KNOW?
STARYU! ATTACK!!
SHYUUU
BOM!
DEAR ME... DO YOU THINK SO?
SHB! SHB! SHB!
WE GOT 'EM!!
IT'S WORKIN'!!

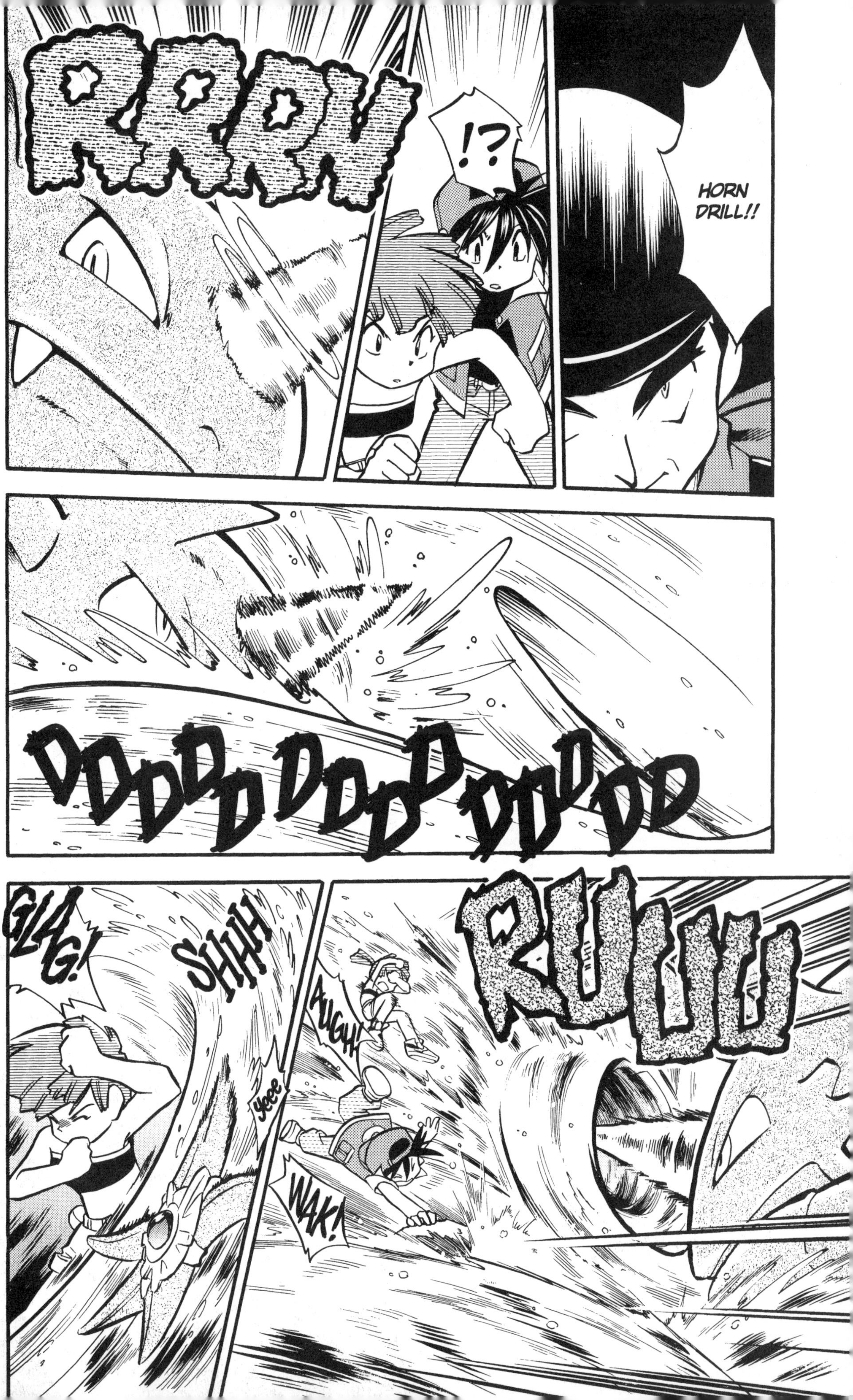
RRRH
!?
HORN DRILL!!
DDDDDDDDDDDDDDD
RUUU
GLAG!
SHHH
AUGH!
YEEE
WAK!

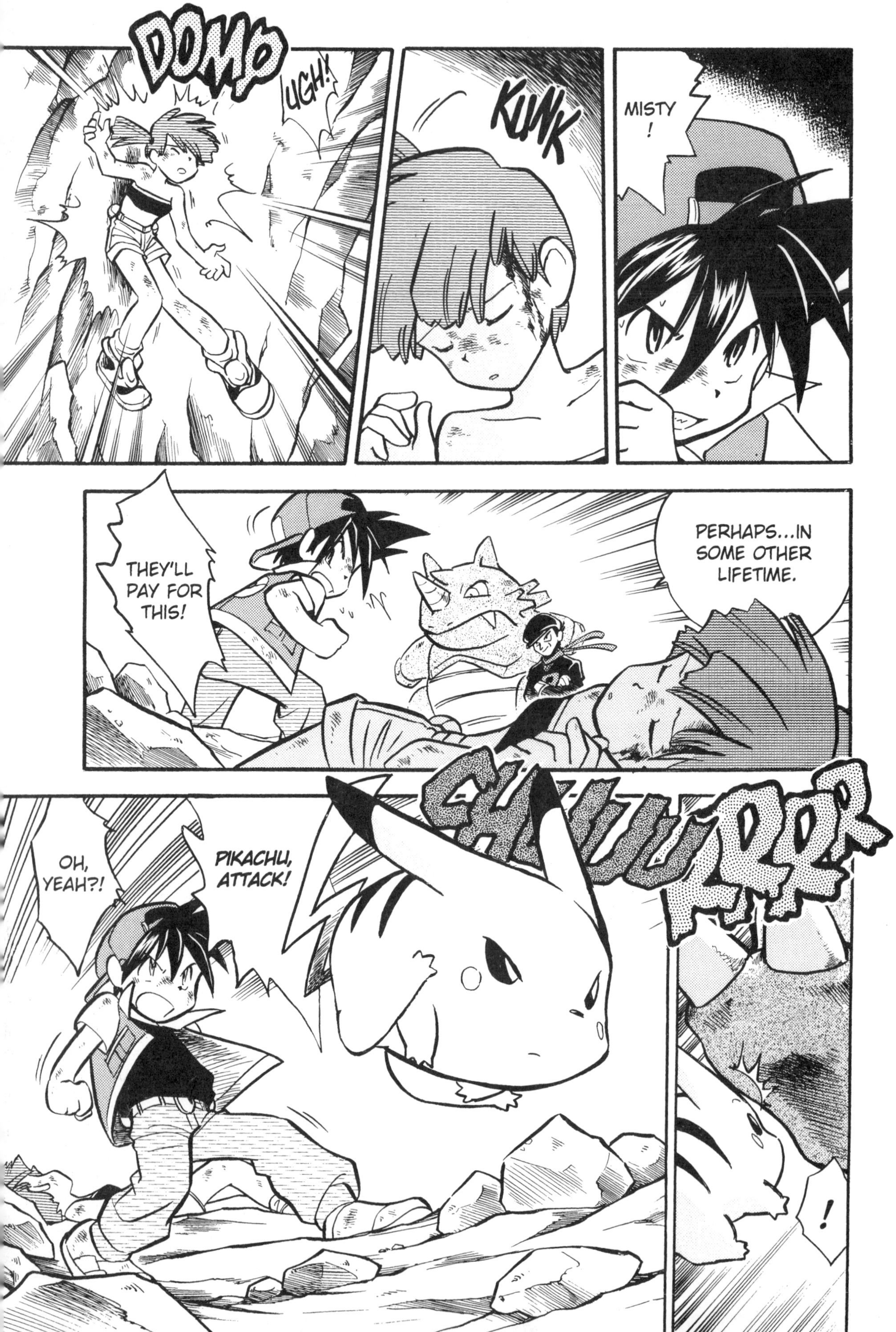
DOMP
UGH!
KUNK
MISTY
!
THEY'LL PAY FOR THIS!
PERHAPS...IN SOME OTHER LIFETIME.
OH, YEAH?!
PIKACHU, ATTACK!
CHUUURRR
!

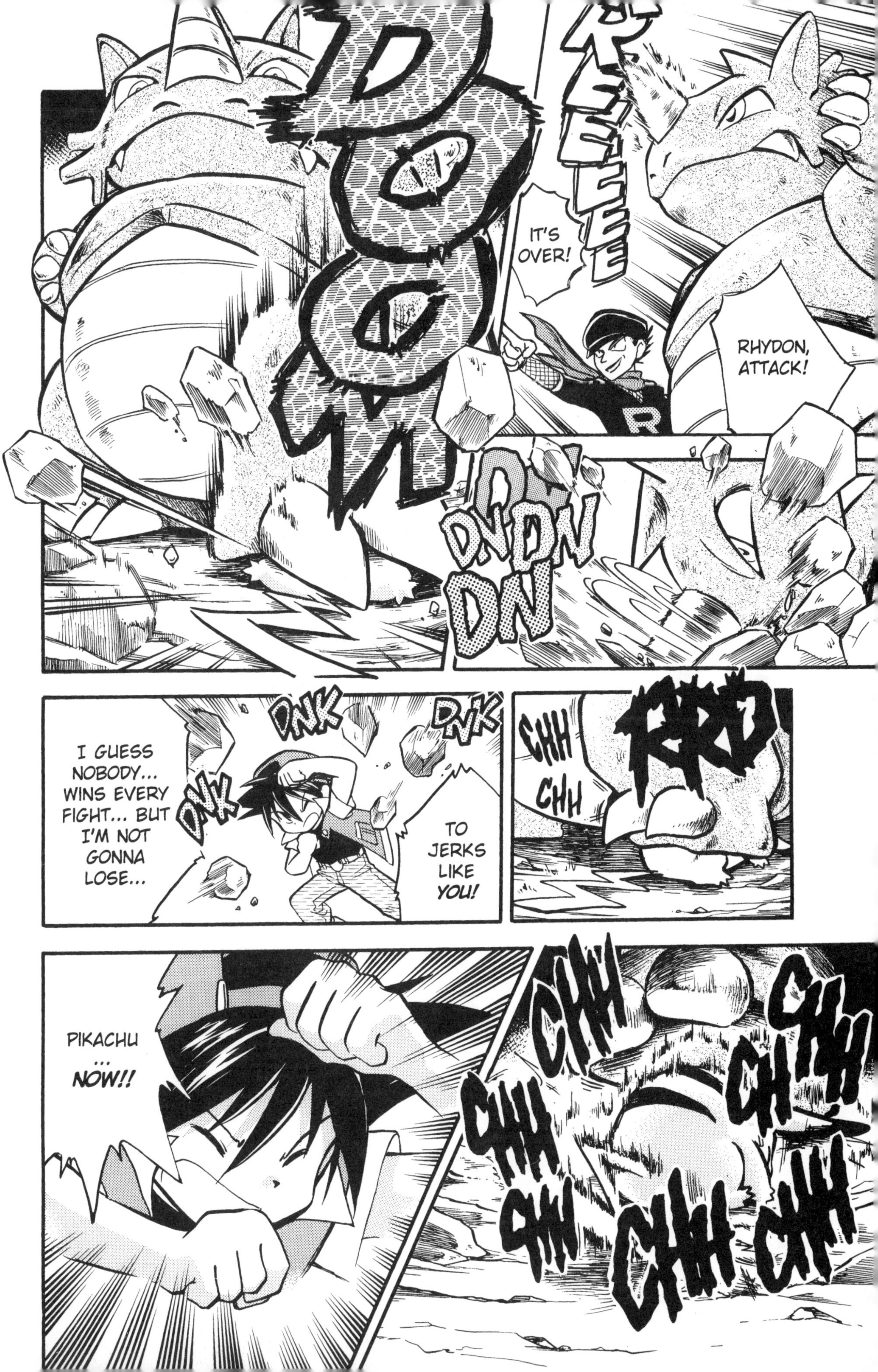
DOOM
REEEEE
IT'S OVER!
RHYDON, ATTACK!
DN DN DN DN
DNK
DNK
I GUESS NOBODY... WINS EVERY FIGHT... BUT I'M NOT GONNA LOSE...
DNK
TO JERKS LIKE YOU!
CHH CHH
RRD
PIKACHU ... NOW!!
CHH CHH CHH CHH CHH CHH CHH CHH

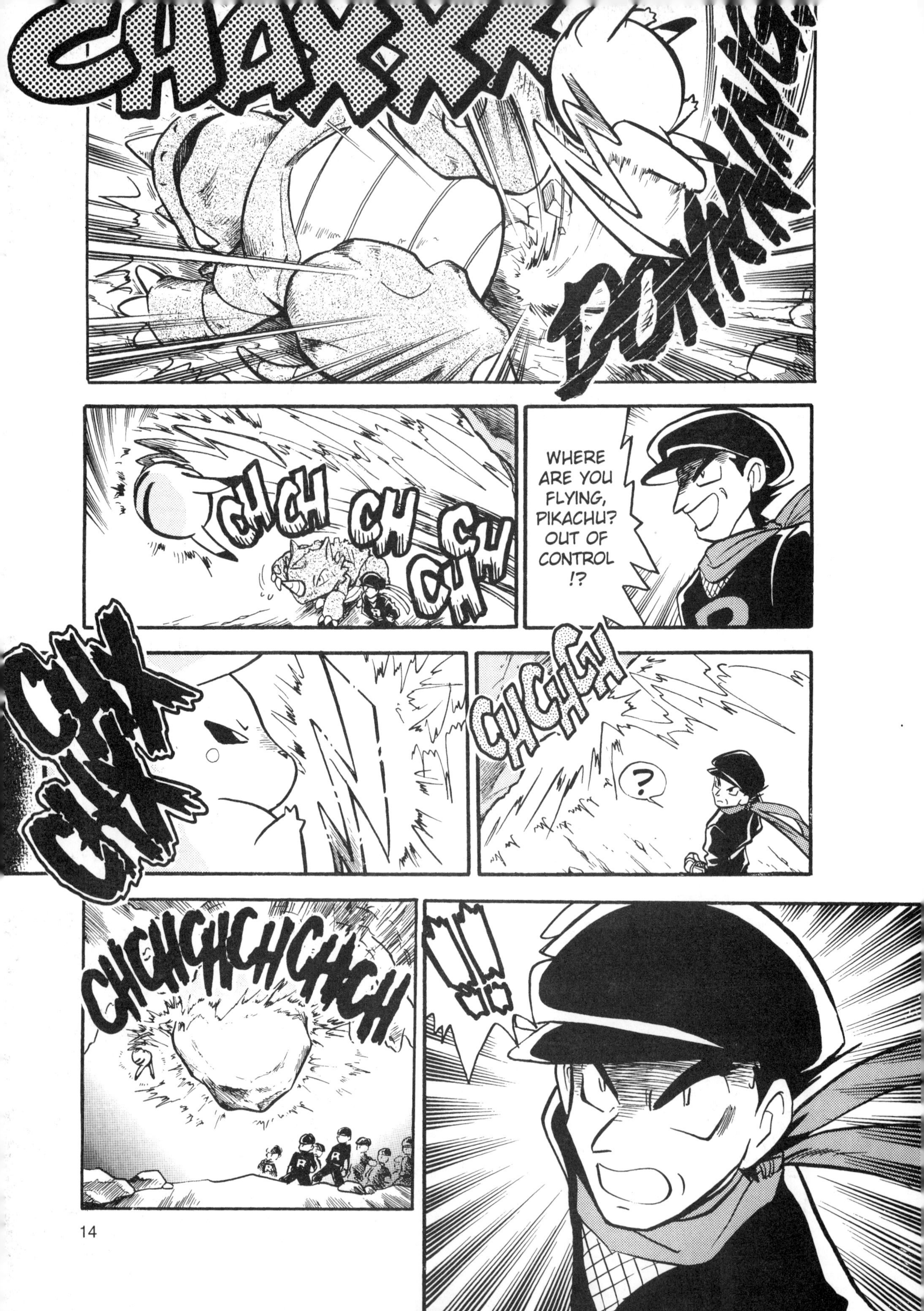
CHAX
DOMMMNG
CHCH CH CH CHCH
WHERE ARE YOU FLYING, PIKACHU? OUT OF CONTROL !?
CHCHCH
CHCHCH
?
CHCHCHCHCHCH
!!

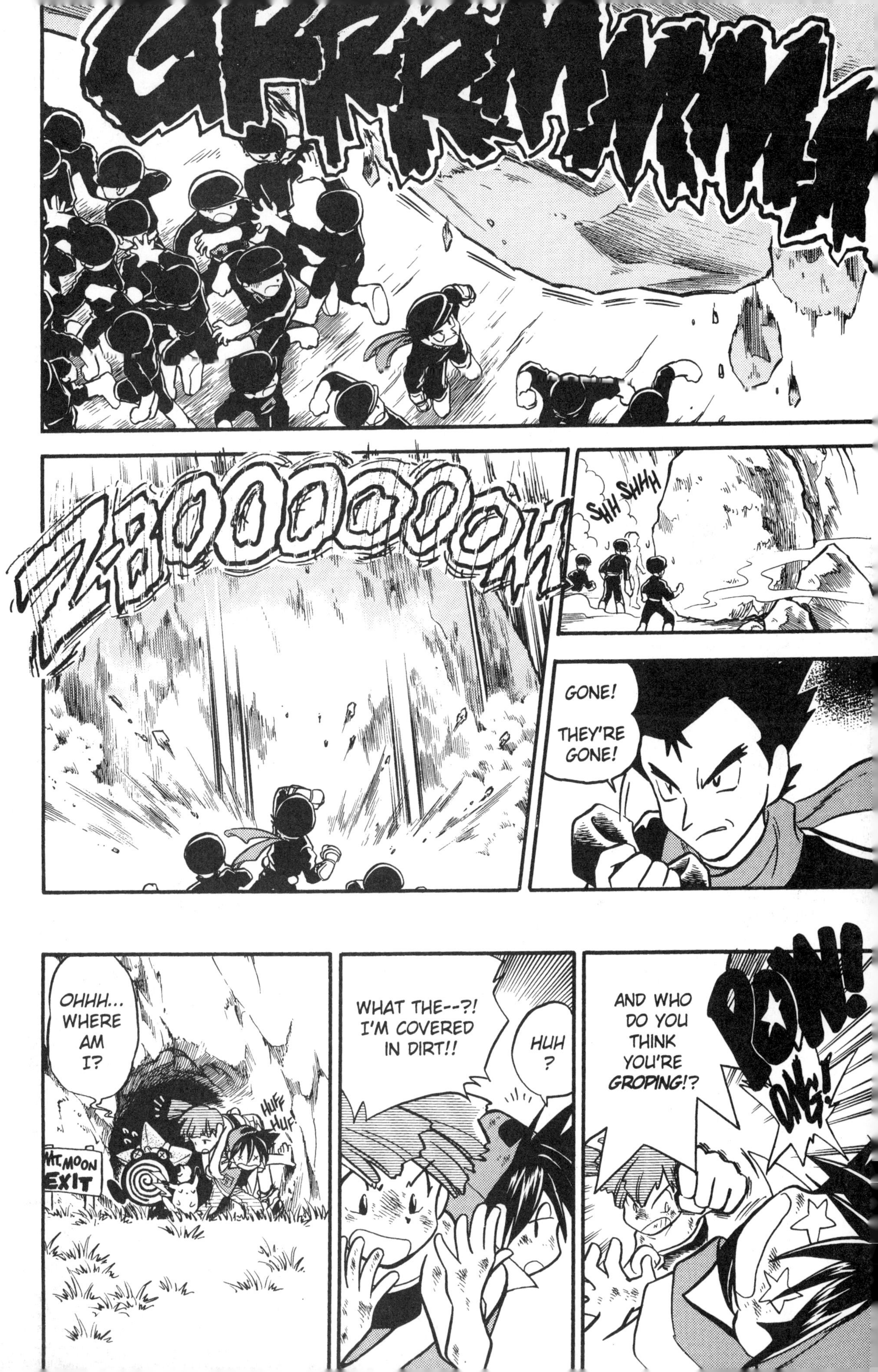
SHH SHHH
GONE!
THEY'RE GONE!
OHHH... WHERE AM I?
HUFF HUF
MOON
EXIT
WHAT THE--?! I'M COVERED IN DIRT!!
HUH ?
AND WHO DO YOU THINK YOU'RE GROPING!?
POW!

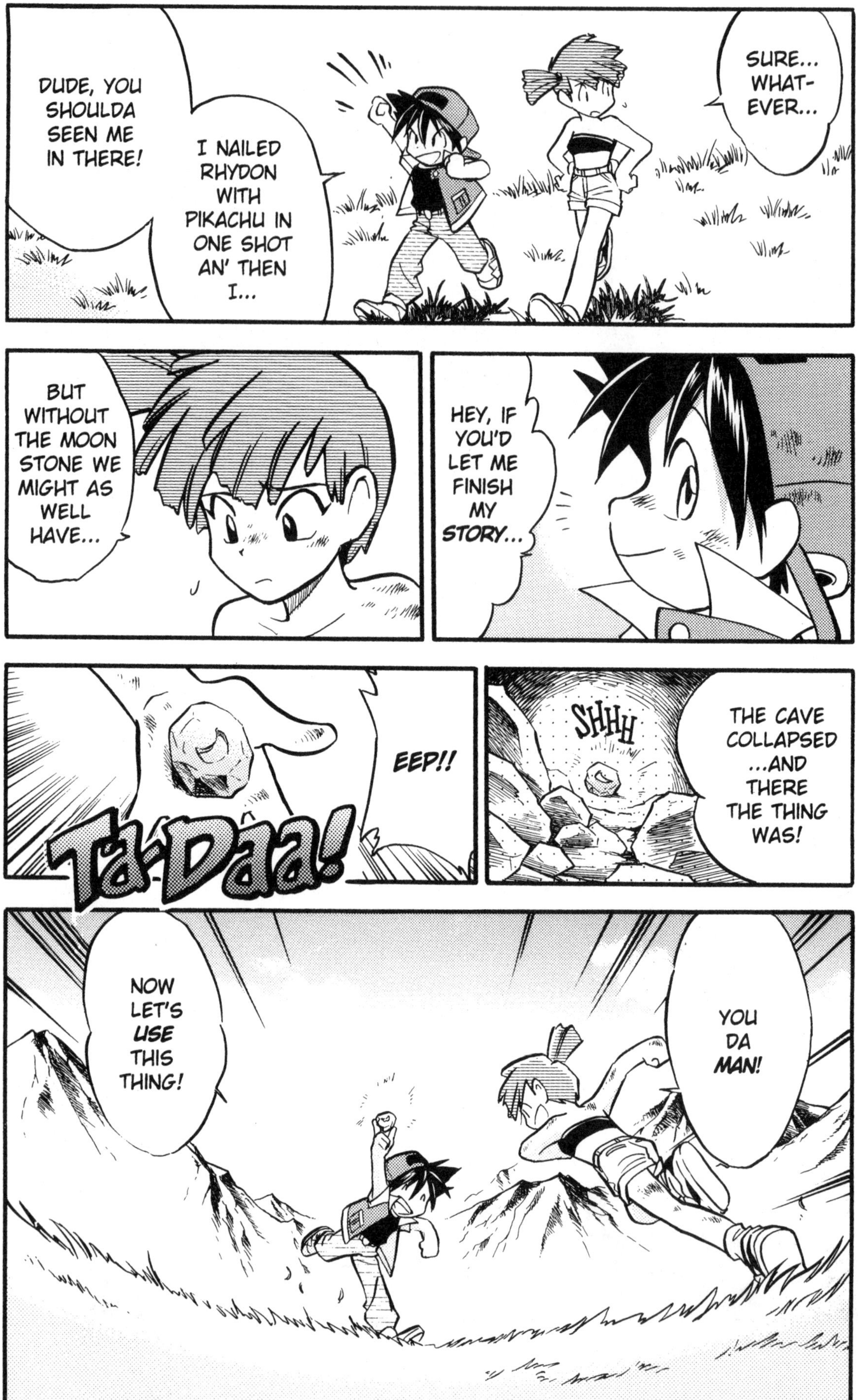
DUDE, YOU SHOULDA SEEN ME IN THERE!
I NAILED RHYDON WITH PIKACHU IN ONE SHOT AN' THEN I...
SURE... WHAT-EVER...
BUT WITHOUT THE MOON STONE WE MIGHT AS WELL HAVE...
HEY, IF YOU'D LET ME FINISH MY STORY...
EEP!!
TA-DAA!
SHHH
THE CAVE COLLAPSED ...AND THERE THE THING WAS!
NOW LET'S USE THIS THING!
YOU DA MAN!

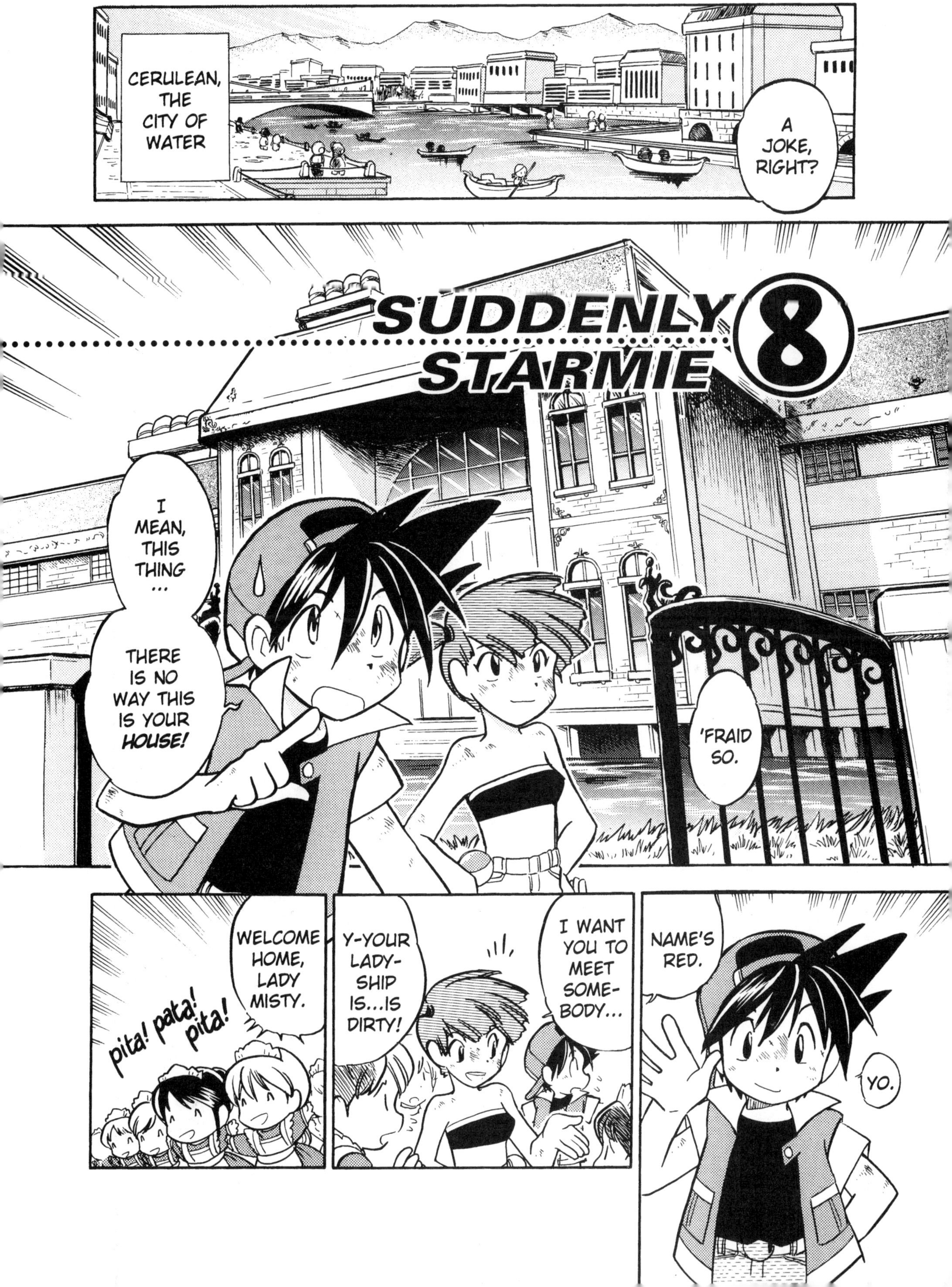
CERULEAN, THE CITY OF WATER
A JOKE, RIGHT?
SUDDENLY STARMIE 8
I MEAN, THIS THING...
THERE IS NO WAY THIS IS YOUR HOUSE!
'FRAID SO.
WELCOME HOME, LADY MISTY.
pita! pata! pita!
Y-YOUR LADYSHIP IS...IS DIRTY!
I WANT YOU TO MEET SOMEBODY...
NAME'S RED.
YO.

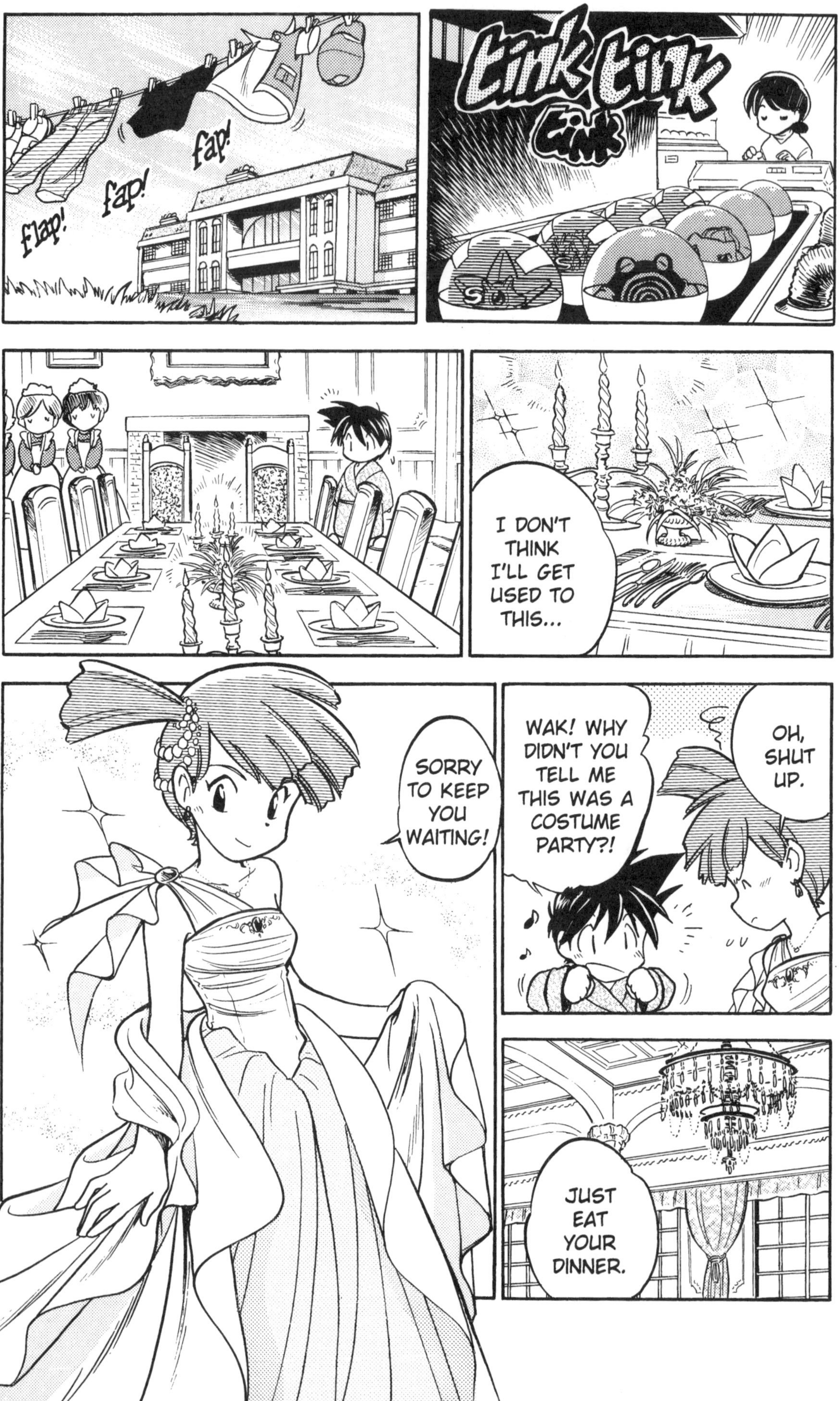
flap!
fap!
fap!
tink tink
tink
I DON'T THINK I'LL GET USED TO THIS...
SORRY TO KEEP YOU WAITING!
WAK! WHY DIDN'T YOU TELL ME THIS WAS A COSTUME PARTY?!
OH, SHUT UP.
JUST EAT YOUR DINNER.

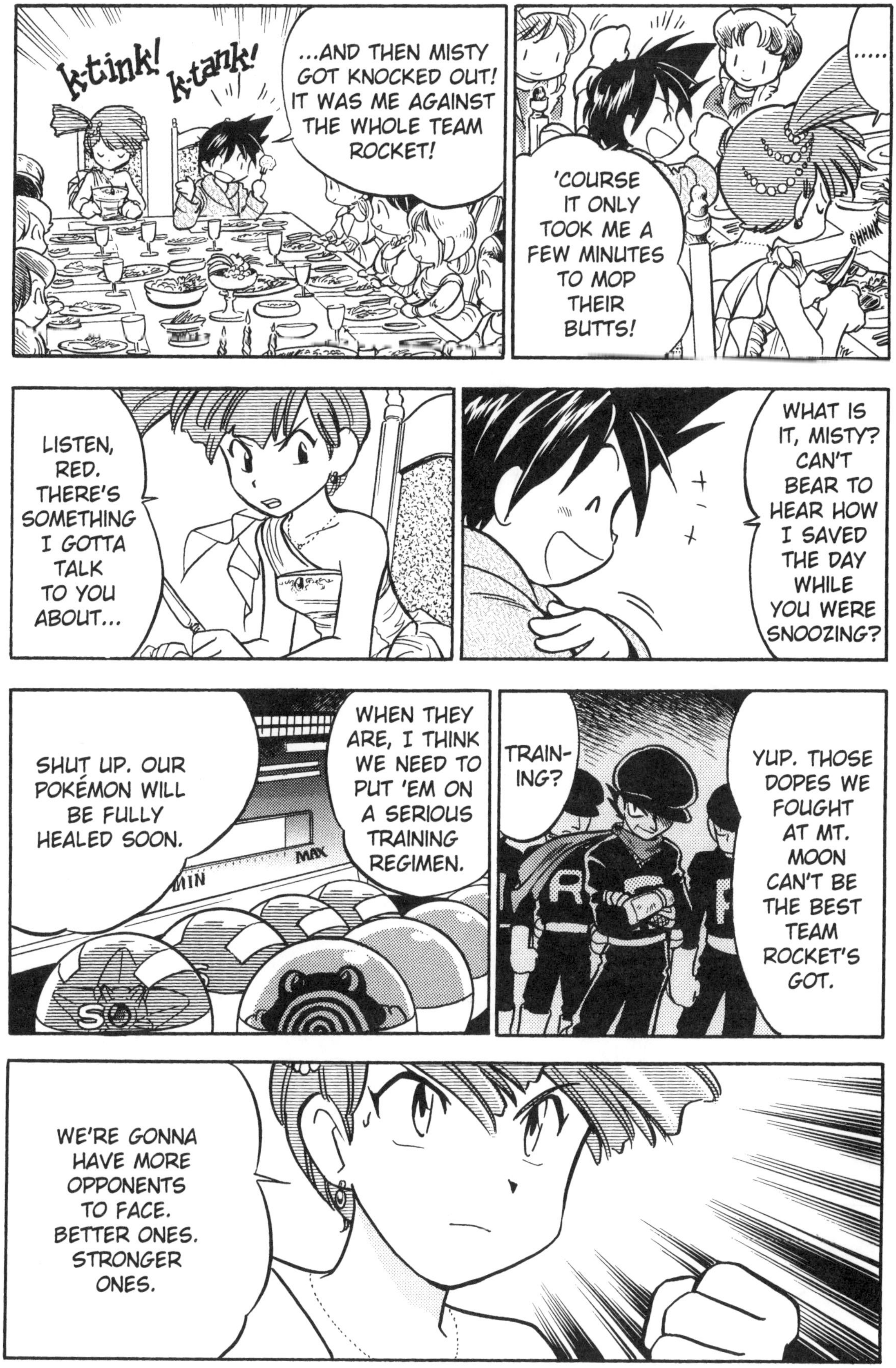
K-TINK! K-TANK!
...AND THEN MISTY GOT KNOCKED OUT! IT WAS ME AGAINST THE WHOLE TEAM ROCKET!
'COURSE IT ONLY TOOK ME A FEW MINUTES TO MOP THEIR BUTTS!
.....
LISTEN, RED. THERE'S SOMETHING I GOTTA TALK TO YOU ABOUT...
WHAT IS IT, MISTY? CAN'T BEAR TO HEAR HOW I SAVED THE DAY WHILE YOU WERE SNOOZING?
SHUT UP. OUR POKÉMON WILL BE FULLY HEALED SOON.
WHEN THEY ARE, I THINK WE NEED TO PUT 'EM ON A SERIOUS TRAINING REGIMEN.
MAX
MIN
TRAIN-ING?
YUP. THOSE DOPES WE FOUGHT AT MT. MOON CAN'T BE THE BEST TEAM ROCKET'S GOT.
WE'RE GONNA HAVE MORE OPPONENTS TO FACE. BETTER ONES. STRONGER ONES.

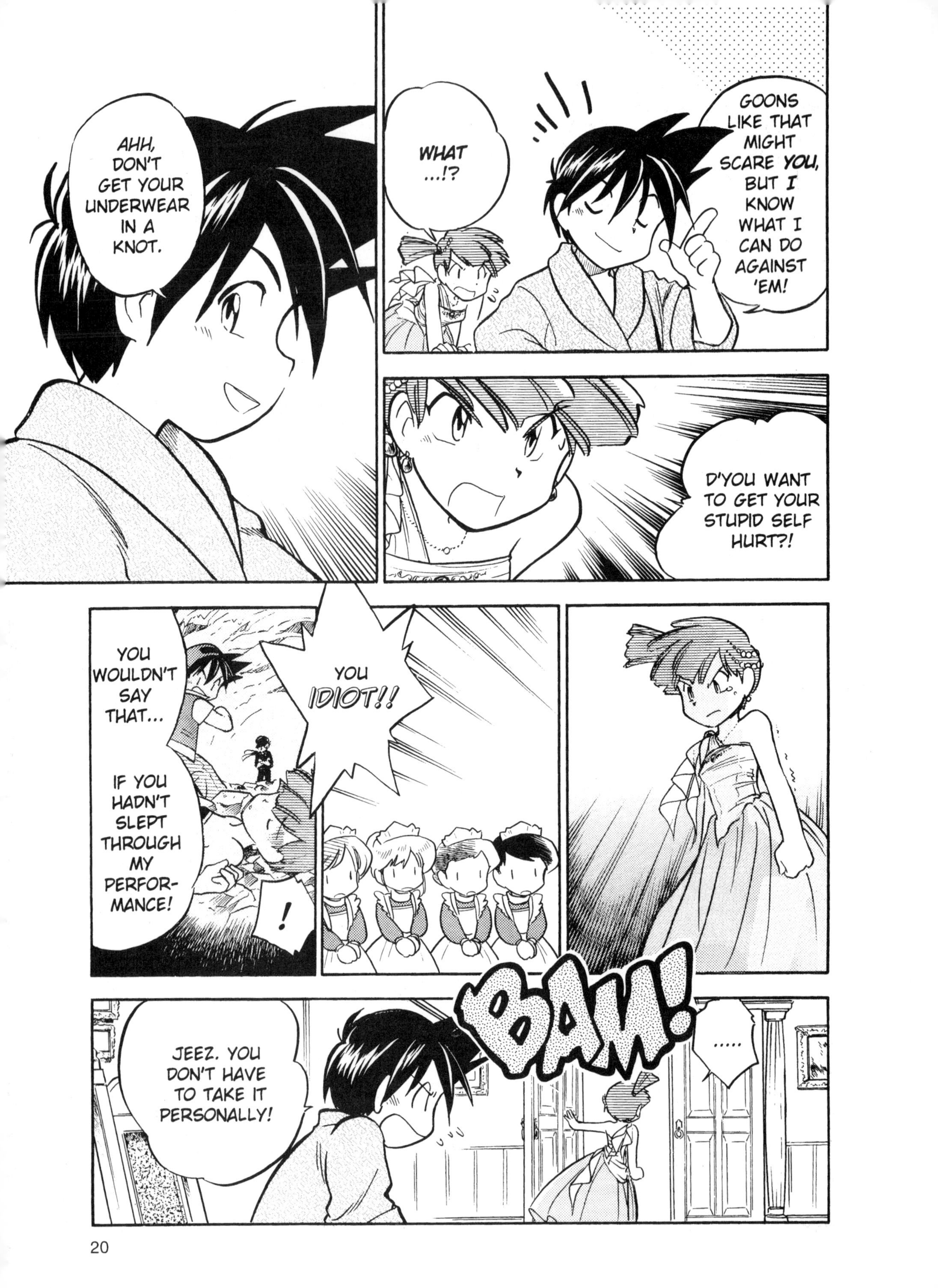

AHH, DON'T GET YOUR UNDERWEAR IN A KNOT.
WHAT ...!?
GOONS LIKE THAT MIGHT SCARE YOU, BUT I KNOW WHAT I CAN DO AGAINST 'EM!
D'YOU WANT TO GET YOUR STUPID SELF HURT?!
YOU IDIOT!!
YOU WOULDN'T SAY THAT...
IF YOU HADN'T SLEPT THROUGH MY PERFORMANCE!
!
BAM!
.....
JEEZ. YOU DON'T HAVE TO TAKE IT PERSONALLY!

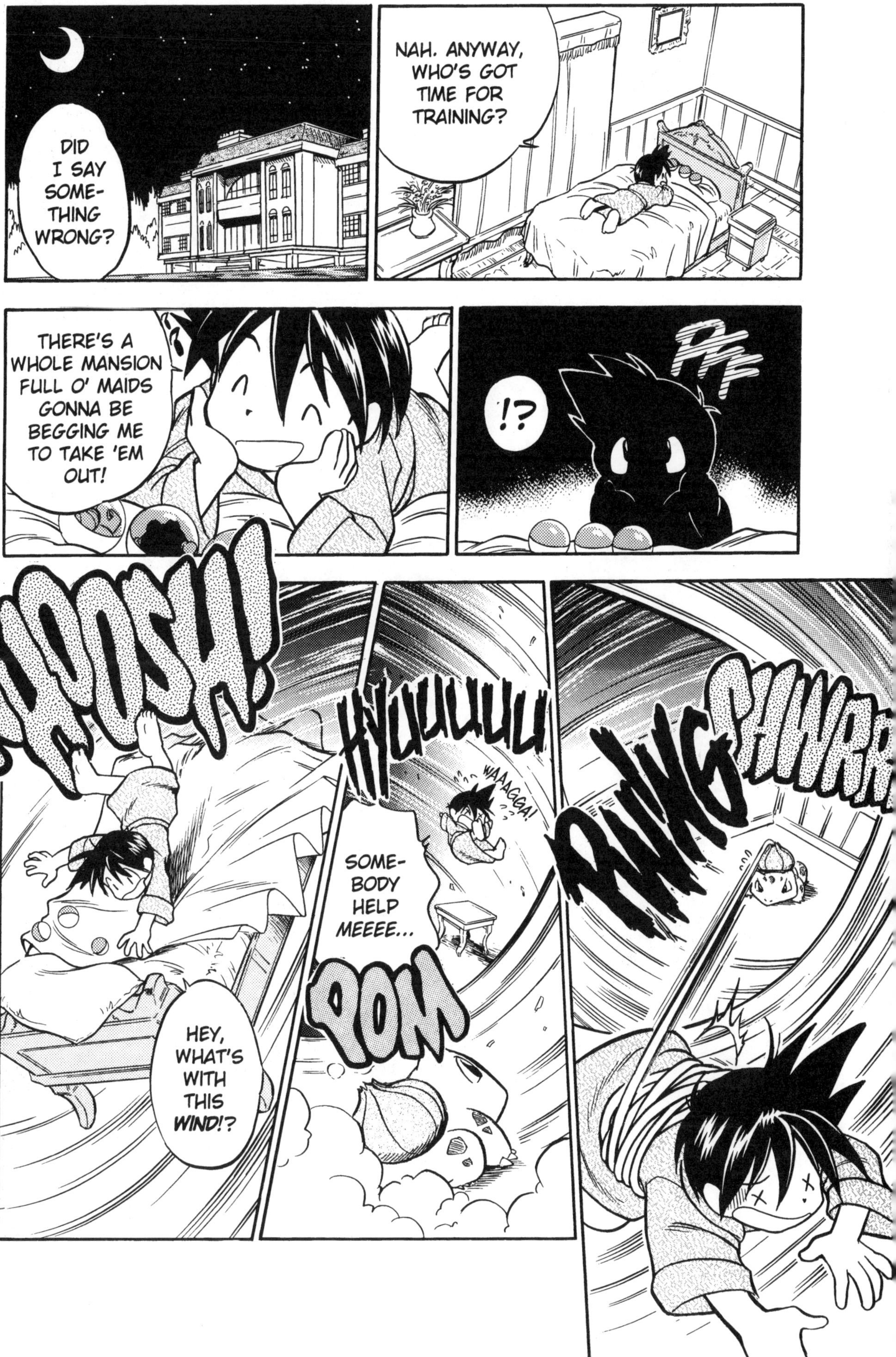
DID I SAY SOME-THING WRONG?
NAH. ANYWAY, WHO'S GOT TIME FOR TRAINING?
THERE'S A WHOLE MANSION FULL O' MAIDS GONNA BE BEGGING ME TO TAKE 'EM OUT!
!?
WHOOSH!
HEY, WHAT'S WITH THIS WIND!?
WAAAGGA!
SOME-BODY HELP MEEEE...
POM

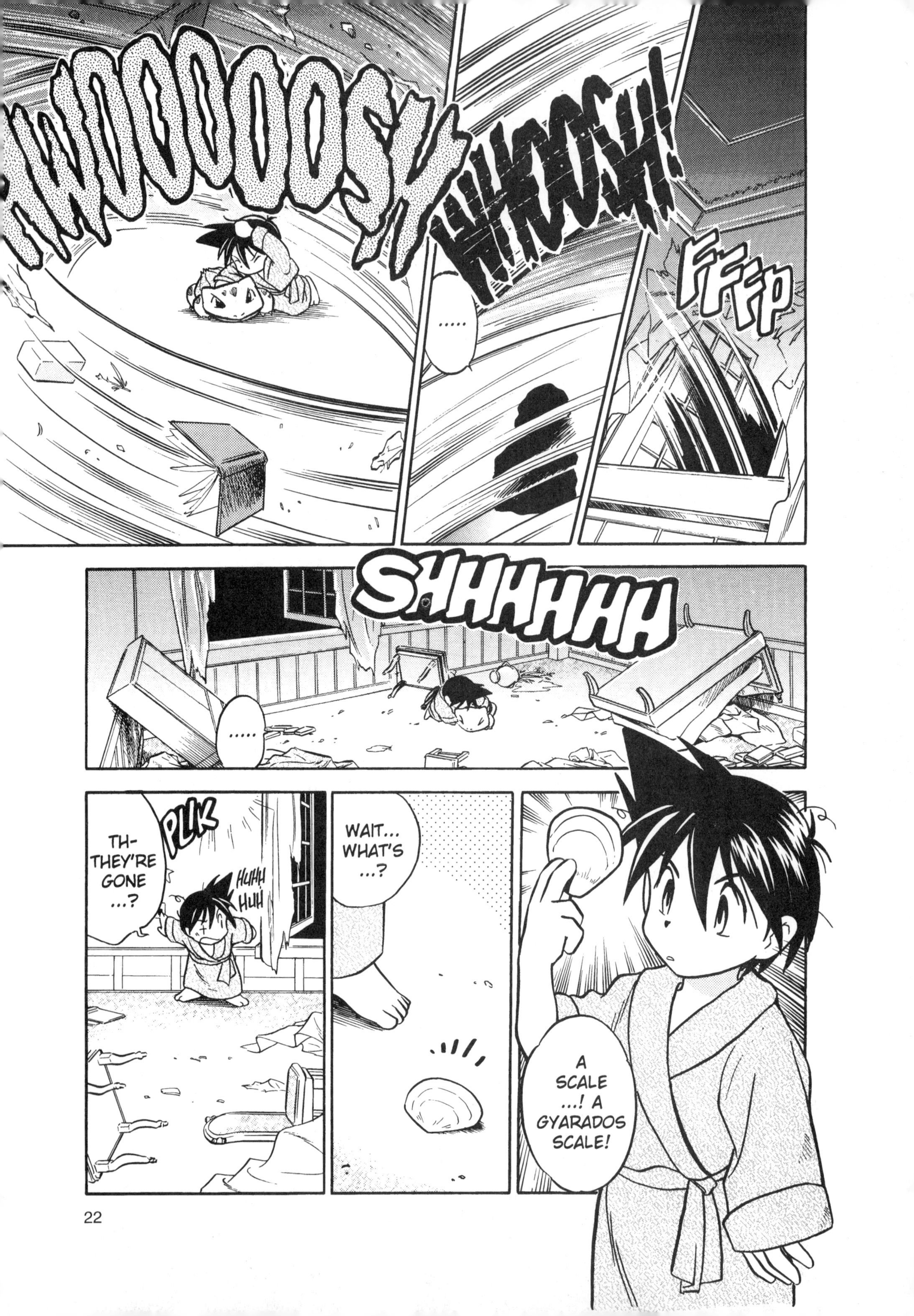
WHOOOOOSH
WHOOSH!
.....
FFFp
SHHHHHH
.....
PLIK
TH- THEY'RE GONE ...?
HUHH HUH
WAIT... WHAT'S ...?
A SCALE ...! A GYARADOS SCALE!

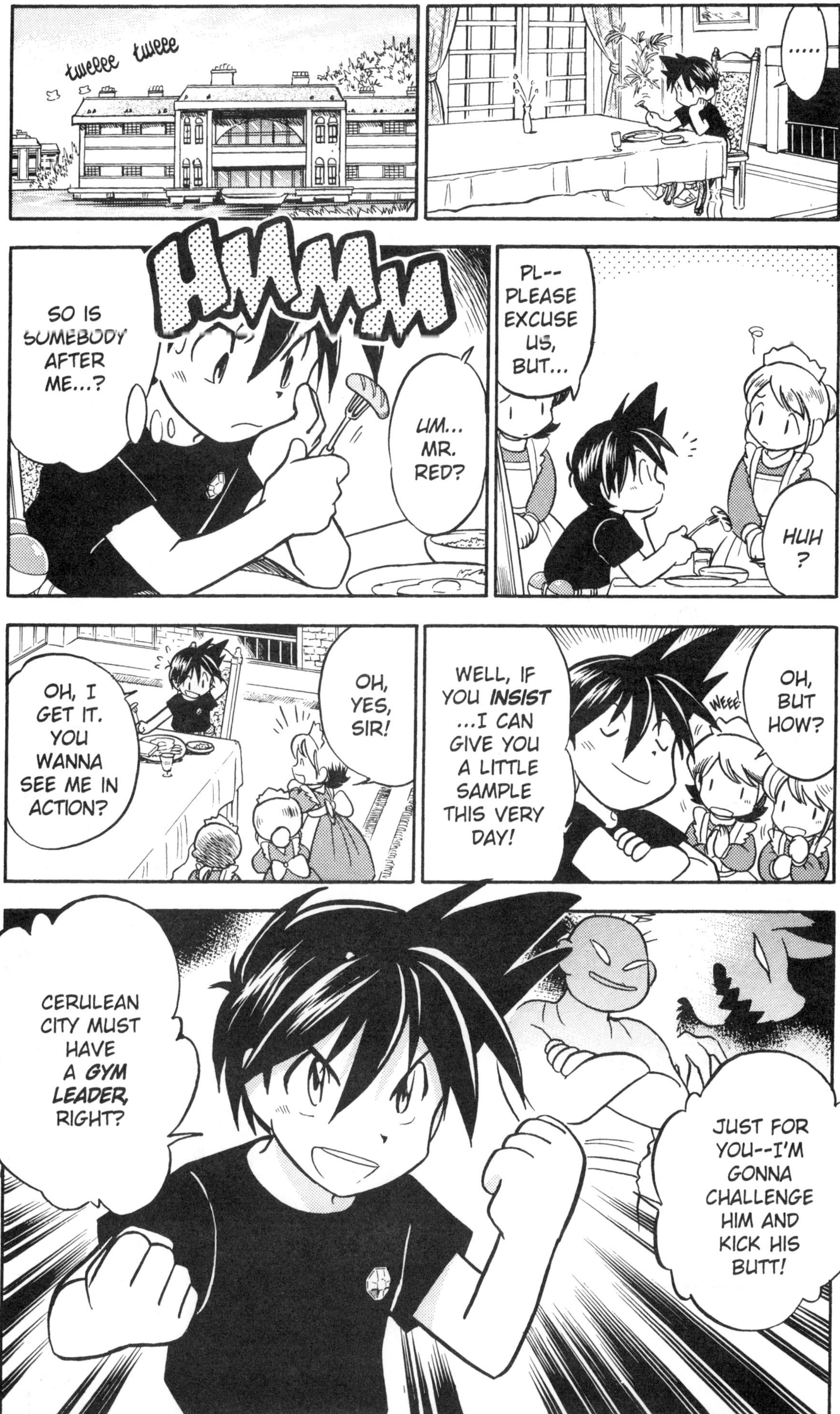
tweee tweee
......
HMMM
SO IS SOMEBODY AFTER ME...?
UM... MR. RED?
PL-- PLEASE EXCUSE US, BUT...
HUH?
OH, I GET IT. YOU WANNA SEE ME IN ACTION?
OH, YES, SIR!
WELL, IF YOU INSIST ...I CAN GIVE YOU A LITTLE SAMPLE THIS VERY DAY!
WEEE!
OH, BUT HOW?
CERULEAN CITY MUST HAVE A GYM LEADER, RIGHT?
JUST FOR YOU--I'M GONNA CHALLENGE HIM AND KICK HIS BUTT!

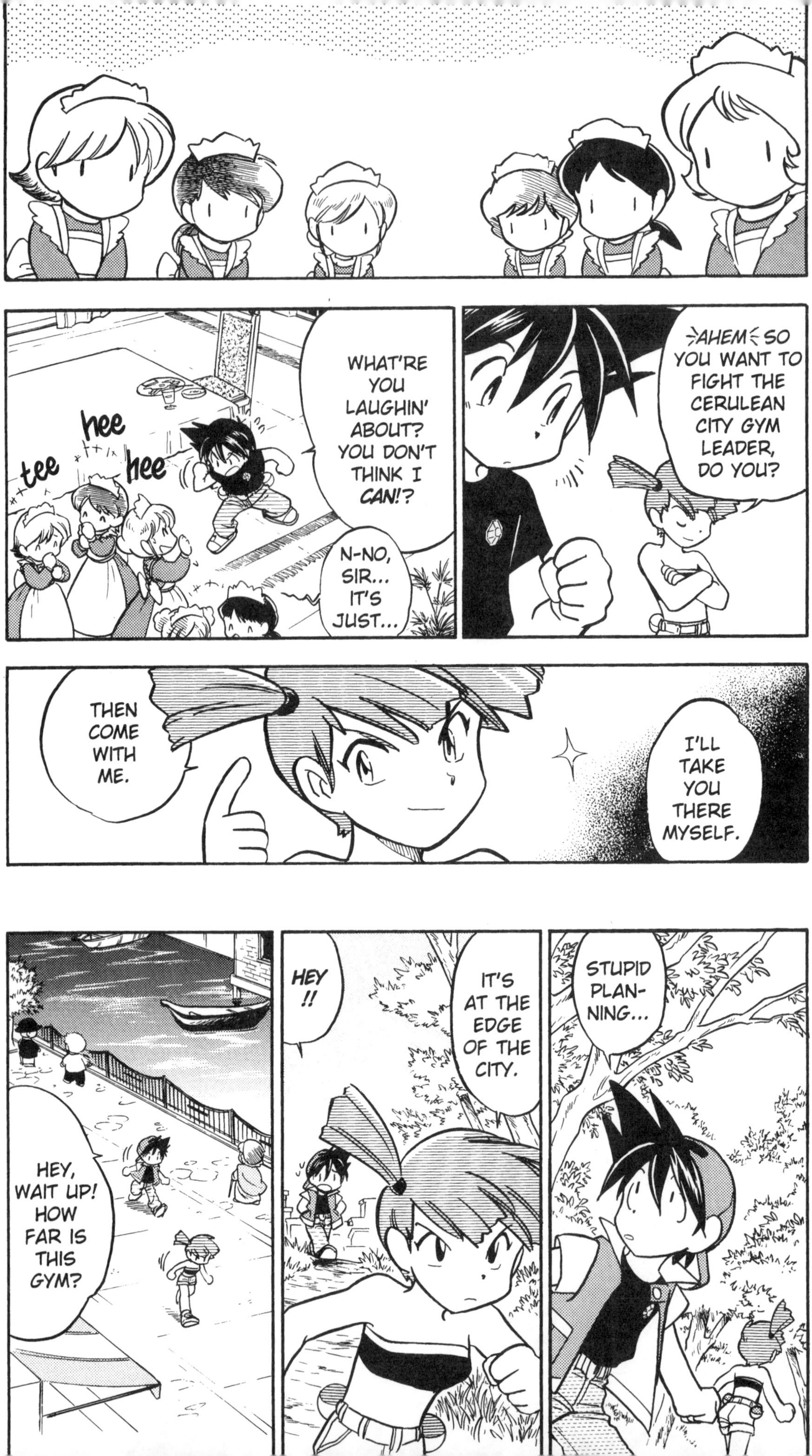
tee
hee
hee
WHAT'RE YOU LAUGHIN' ABOUT? YOU DON'T THINK I *CAN!*?
N-NO, SIR... IT'S JUST...
AHEM SO YOU WANT TO FIGHT THE CERULEAN CITY GYM LEADER, DO YOU?
THEN COME WITH ME.
I'LL TAKE YOU THERE MYSELF.
HEY, WAIT UP! HOW FAR IS THIS GYM?
HEY !!
IT'S AT THE EDGE OF THE CITY.
STUPID PLAN-NING...

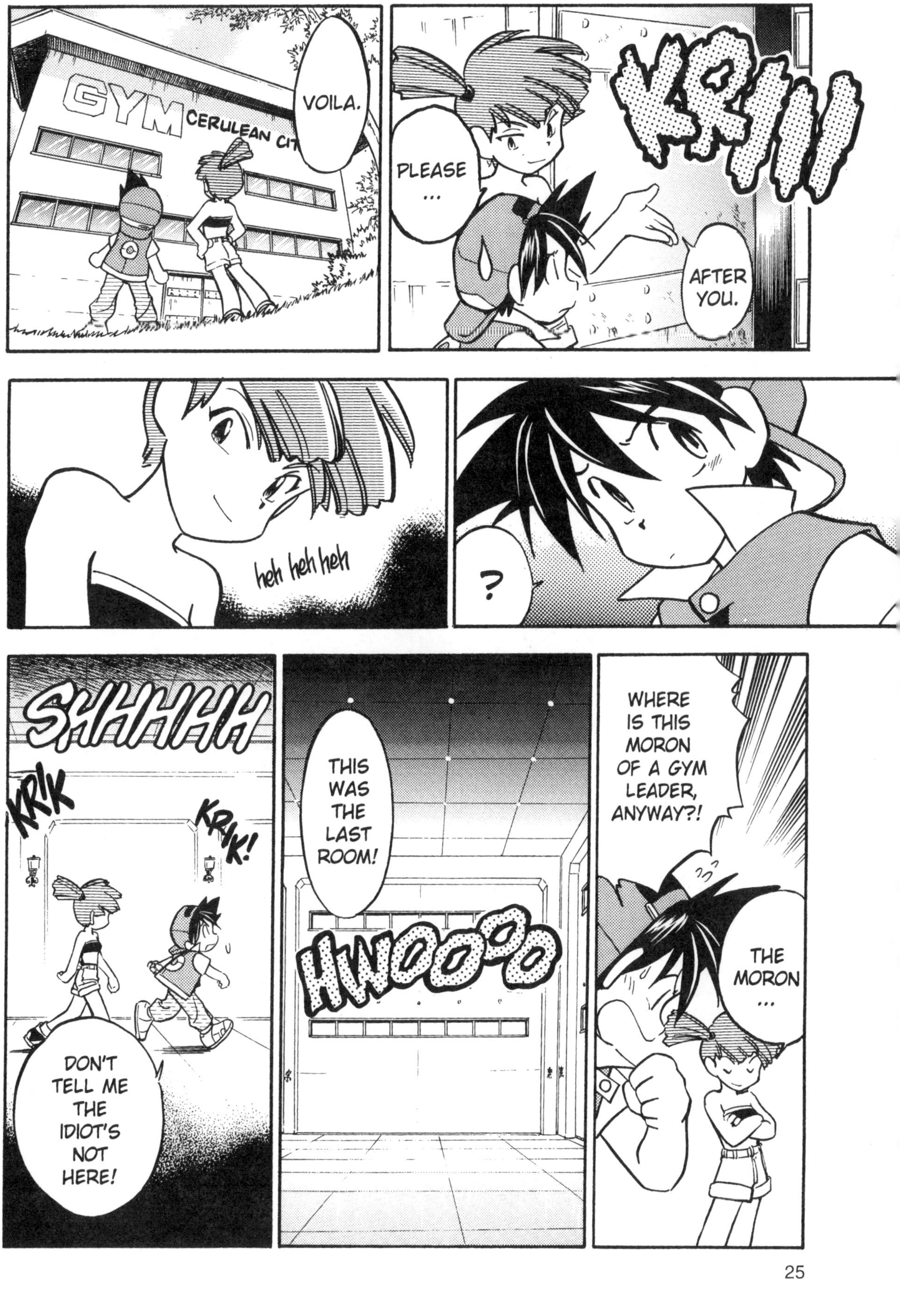
GYM
CERULEAN CIT
VOILA.
PLEASE ...
KRIII
AFTER YOU.
heh heh heh
?
SHHHHH
KRIK
KRIK!
DON'T TELL ME THE IDIOT'S NOT HERE!
THIS WAS THE LAST ROOM!
HWOOOO
WHERE IS THIS MORON OF A GYM LEADER, ANYWAY?!
THE MORON ...

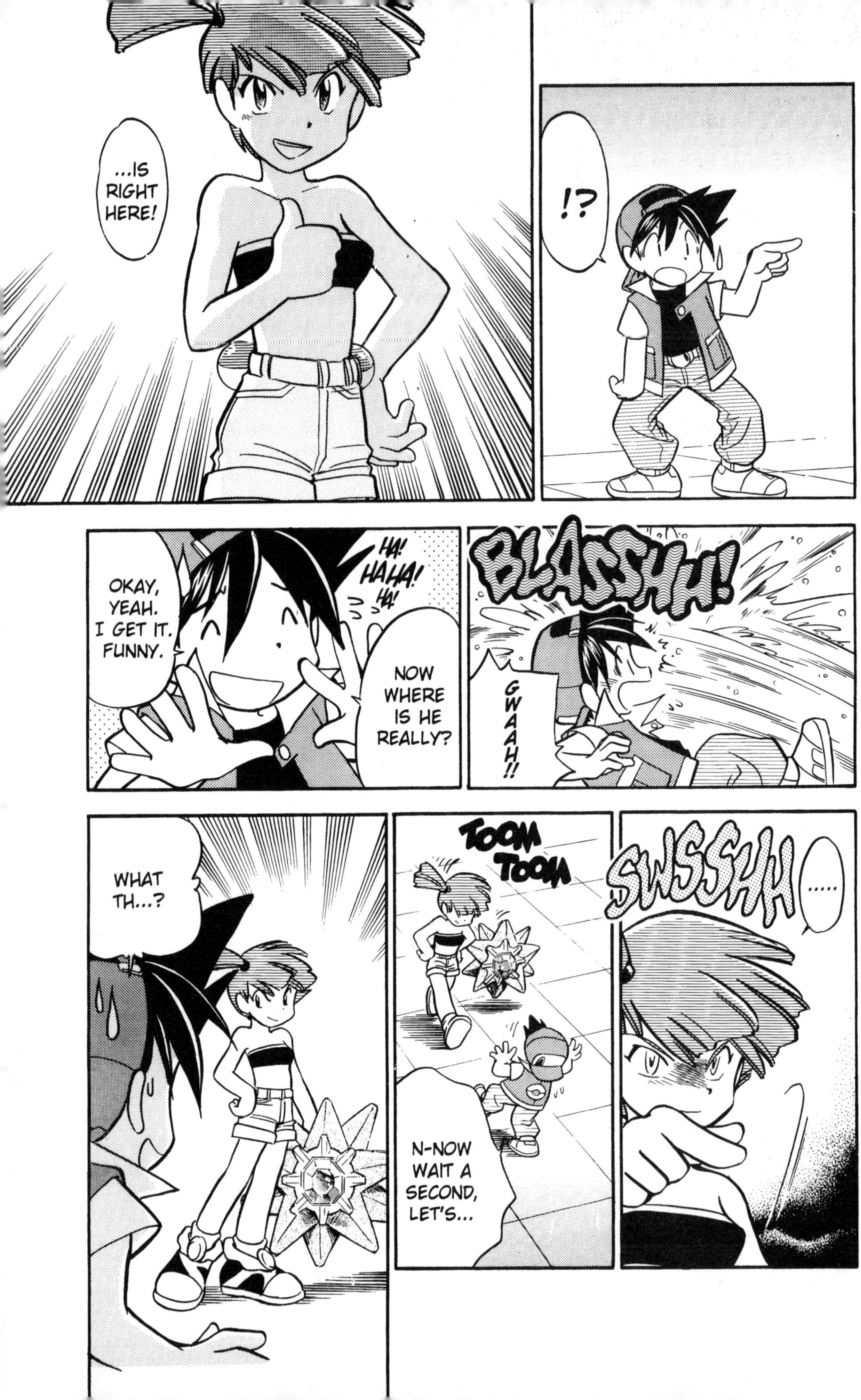
...IS RIGHT HERE!
!?
OKAY, YEAH. I GET IT. FUNNY.
HA! HAHA! HA!
NOW WHERE IS HE REALLY?
BLASSHH!
GWAAAH!!
WHAT TH...?
TOOM TOOM
N-NOW WAIT A SECOND, LET'S...
SWSSHH
.....

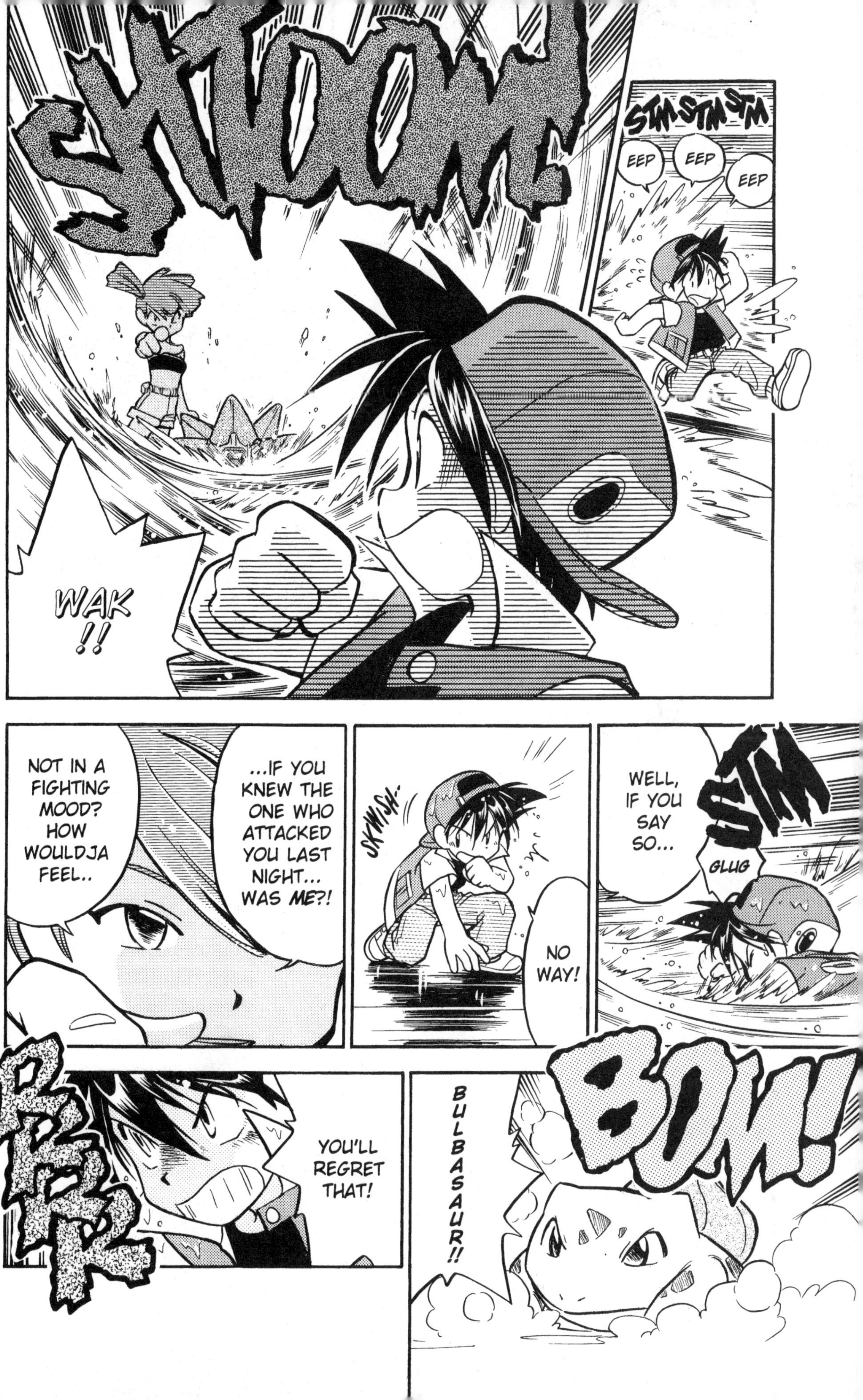
SHOOM!
STM STM STM
EEP
EEP
EEP
WAK !!
NOT IN A FIGHTING MOOD? HOW WOULDJA FEEL..
...IF YOU KNEW THE ONE WHO ATTACKED YOU LAST NIGHT... WAS ME?!
SKWISH
NO WAY!
WELL, IF YOU SAY SO...
STM
GLUG
RRR
YOU'LL REGRET THAT!
BULBASAUR!!
BOM!!

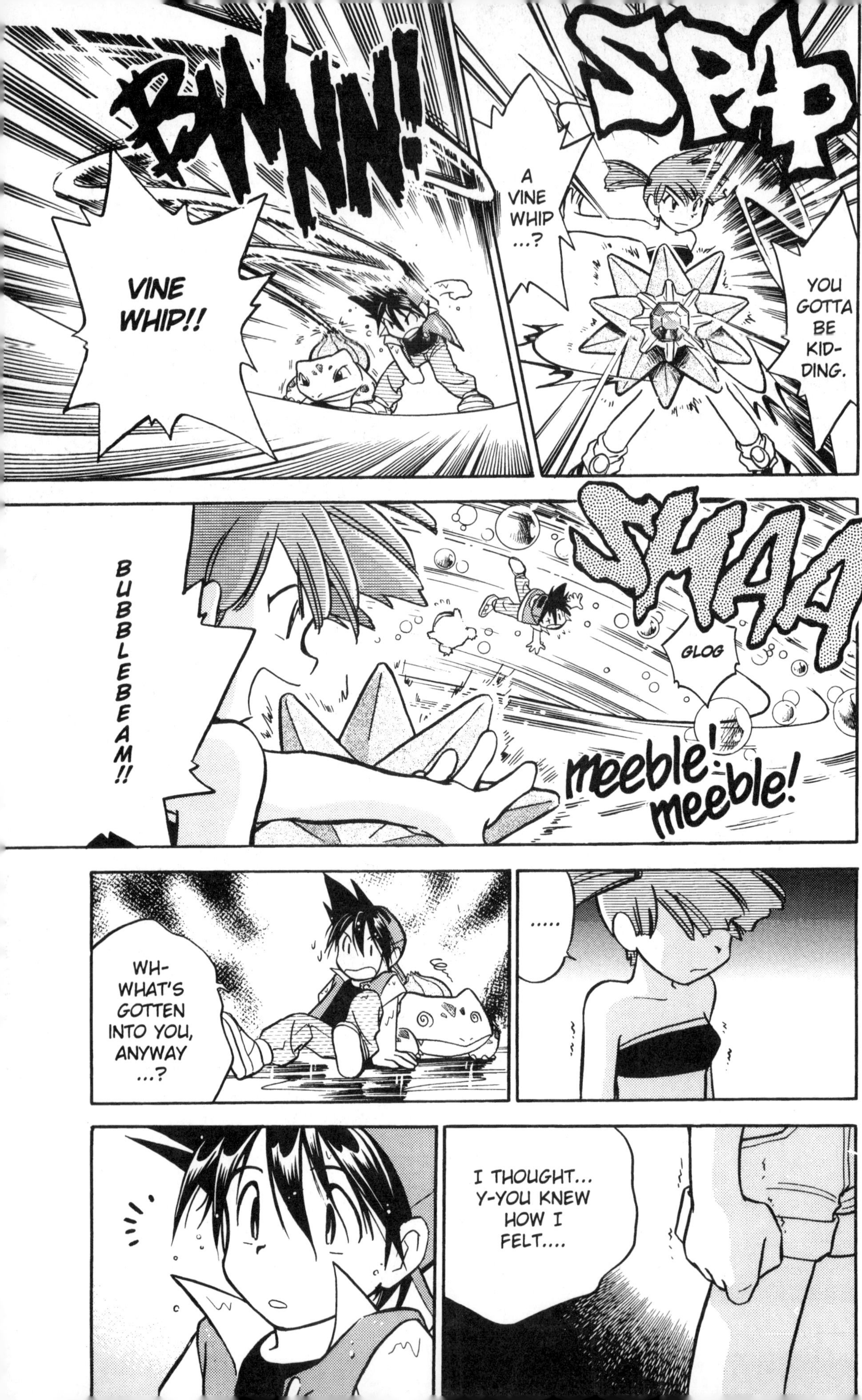
BMNN!
VINE WHIP!!
SPAP
A VINE WHIP ...?
YOU GOTTA BE KID-DING.
SHAA
BUBBLEBEAM!!
GLOG
meeble! meeble!
WH-WHAT'S GOTTEN INTO YOU, ANYWAY ...?
.....
I THOUGHT... Y-YOU KNEW HOW I FELT....

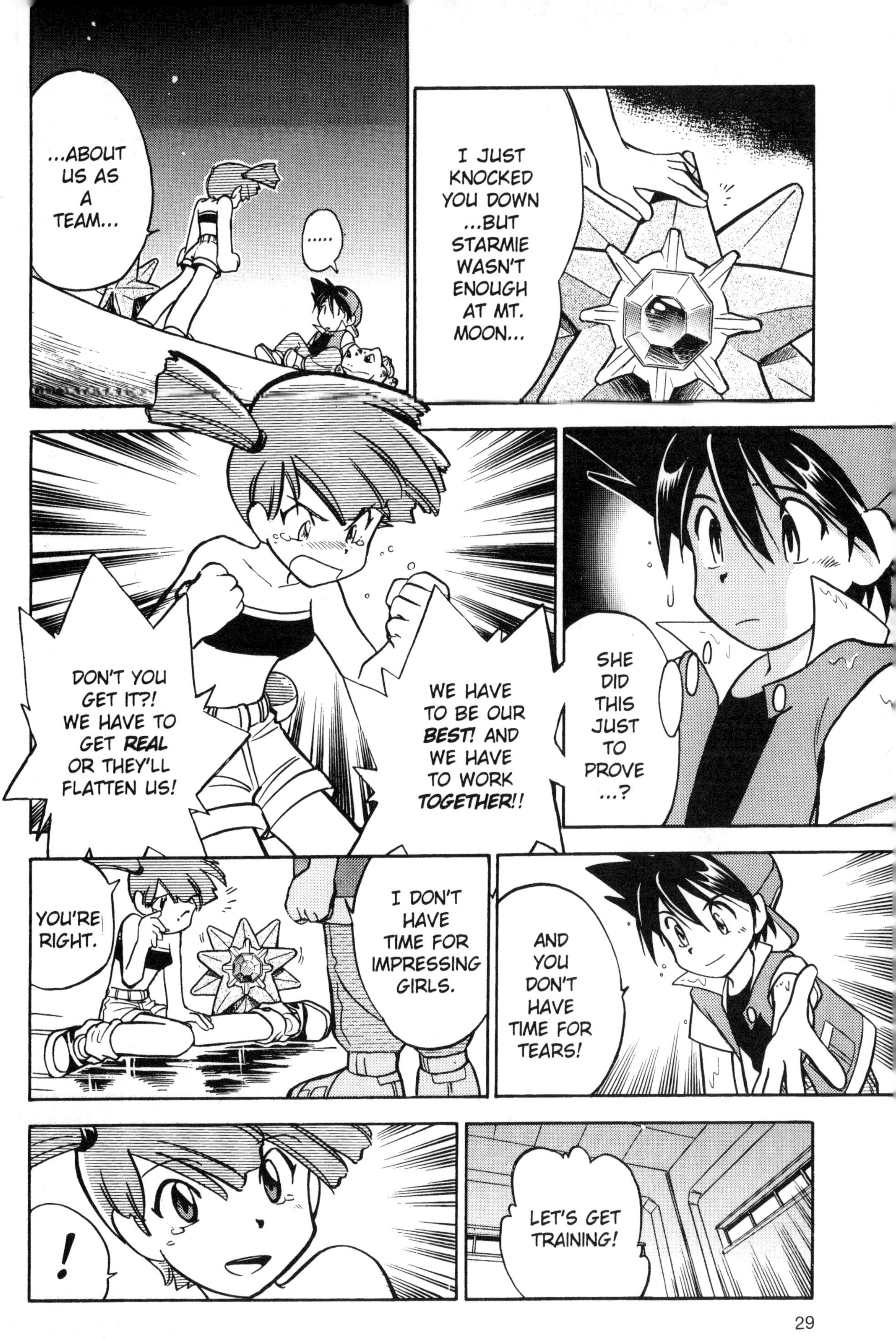

...ABOUT US AS A TEAM...
.....
I JUST KNOCKED YOU DOWN ...BUT STARMIE WASN'T ENOUGH AT MT. MOON...
DON'T YOU GET IT?! WE HAVE TO GET REAL OR THEY'LL FLATTEN US!
WE HAVE TO BE OUR BEST! AND WE HAVE TO WORK TOGETHER!!
SHE DID THIS JUST TO PROVE ...?
YOU'RE RIGHT.
I DON'T HAVE TIME FOR IMPRESSING GIRLS.
AND YOU DON'T HAVE TIME FOR TEARS!
!
LET'S GET TRAINING!

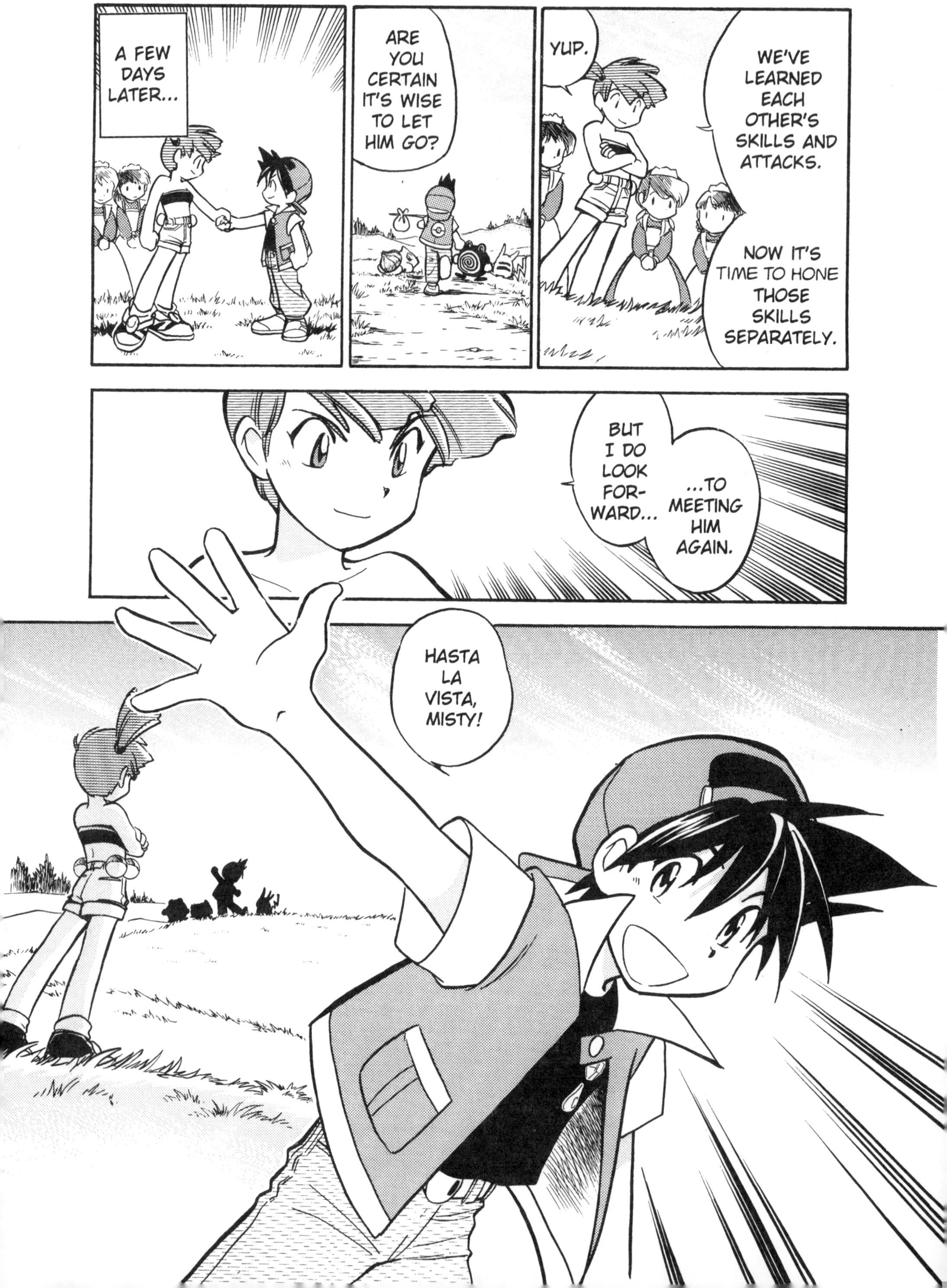
A FEW DAYS LATER...
ARE YOU CERTAIN IT'S WISE TO LET HIM GO?
YUP.
WE'VE LEARNED EACH OTHER'S SKILLS AND ATTACKS.
NOW IT'S TIME TO HONE THOSE SKILLS SEPARATELY.
BUT I DO LOOK FOR-WARD...
...TO MEETING HIM AGAIN.
HASTA LA VISTA, MISTY!

CHAPTER 9

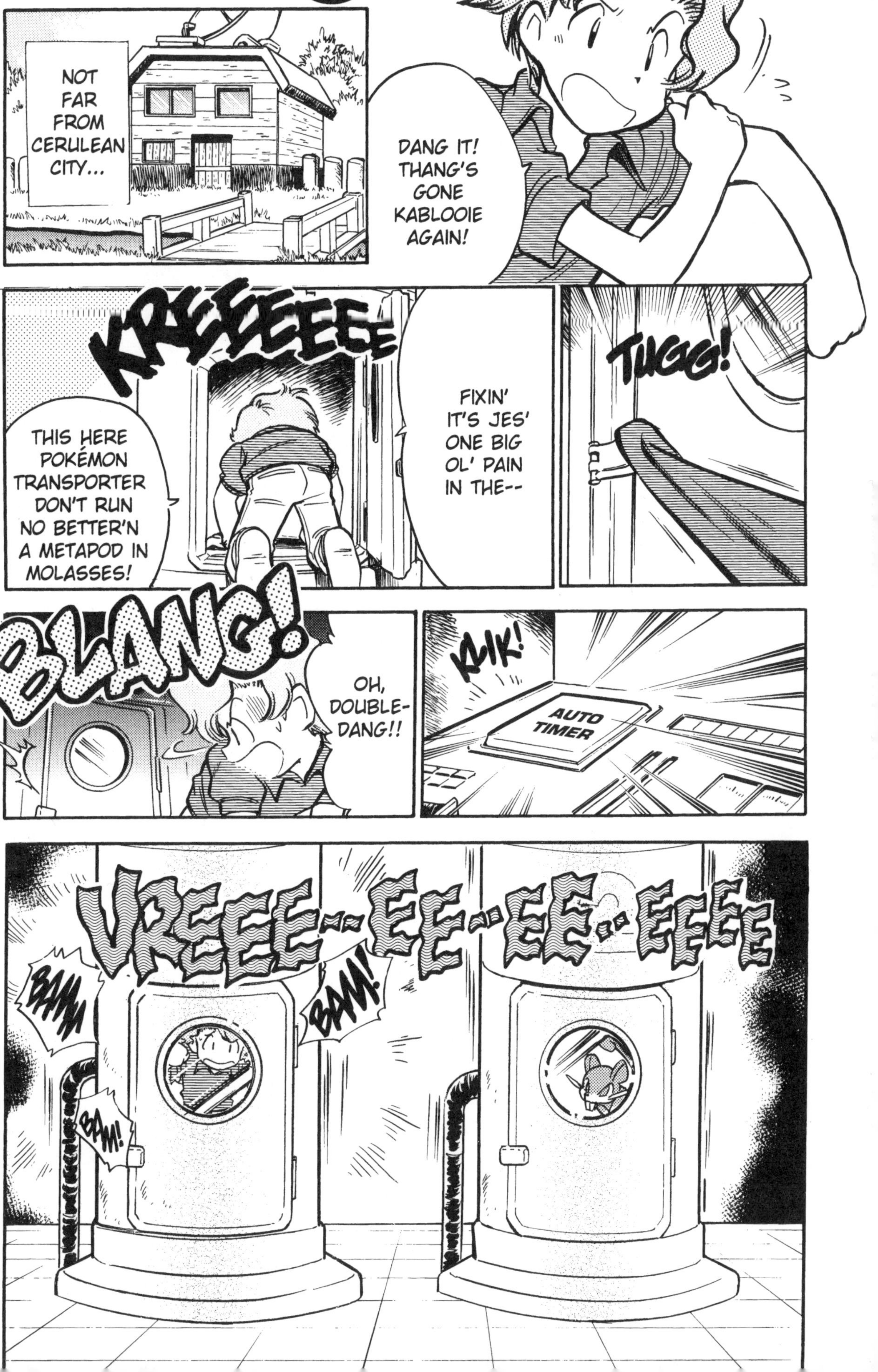
NOT FAR FROM CERULEAN CITY...
DANG IT! THANG'S GONE KABLOOIE AGAIN!
KREEEEEE
THIS HERE POKÉMON TRANSPORTER DON'T RUN NO BETTER'N A METAPOD IN MOLASSES!
FIXIN' IT'S JES' ONE BIG OL' PAIN IN THE--
TUGG!
BLANG!
OH, DOUBLE-DANG!!
KLIK!
AUTO TIMER
VREEE--EE--EE--EEEE
BAMM
BAM!
BAM!

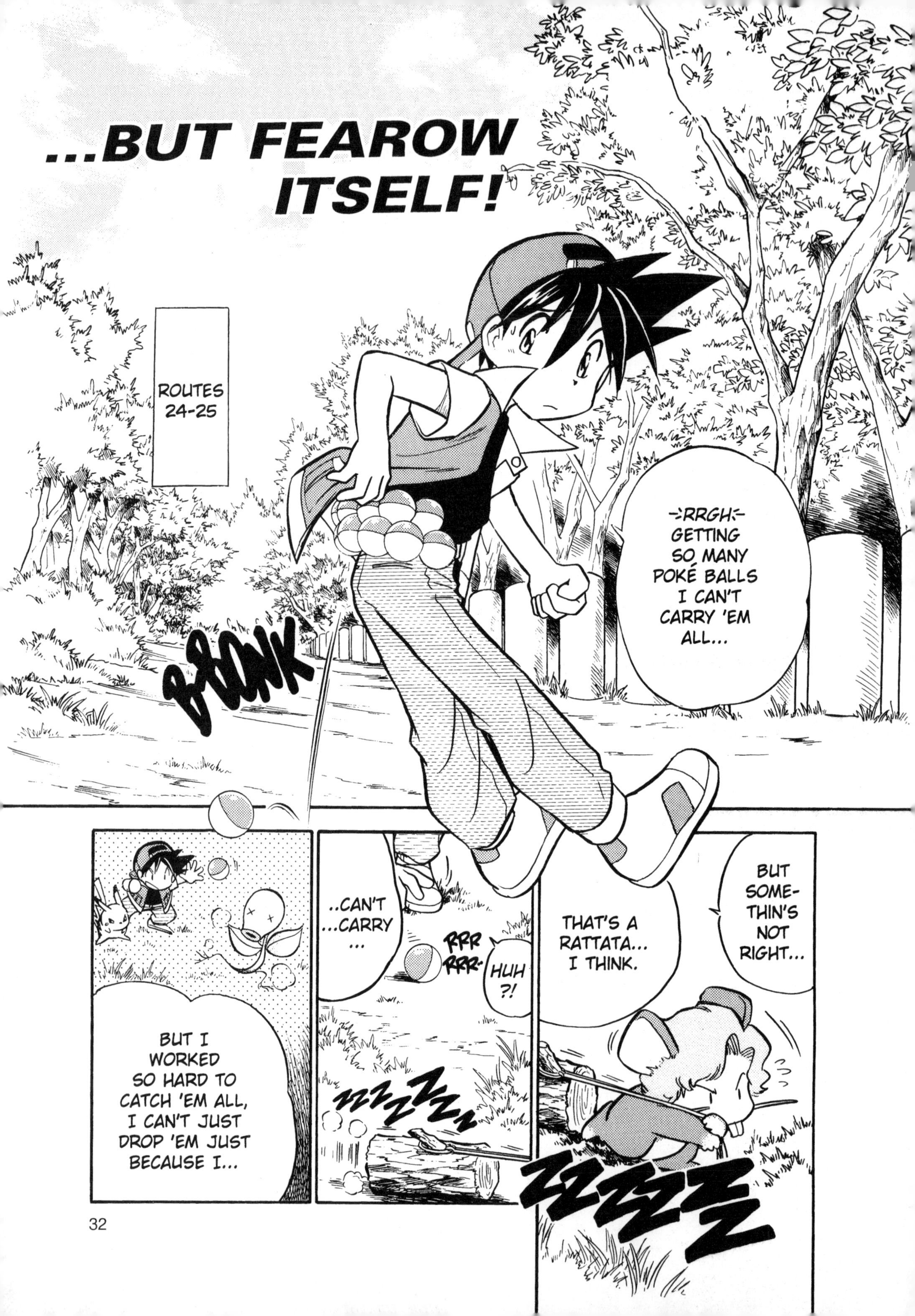

...BUT FEAROW ITSELF!
ROUTES 24-25
-RRGH- GETTING SO MANY POKÉ BALLS I CAN'T CARRY 'EM ALL...
BDONK
BUT I WORKED SO HARD TO CATCH 'EM ALL, I CAN'T JUST DROP 'EM JUST BECAUSE I...
..CAN'T ...CARRY ...
RRR RRR
HUH ?!
ZZZZZZZZ
BUT SOME-THIN'S NOT RIGHT...
THAT'S A RATTATA... I THINK.
ZZZZZ

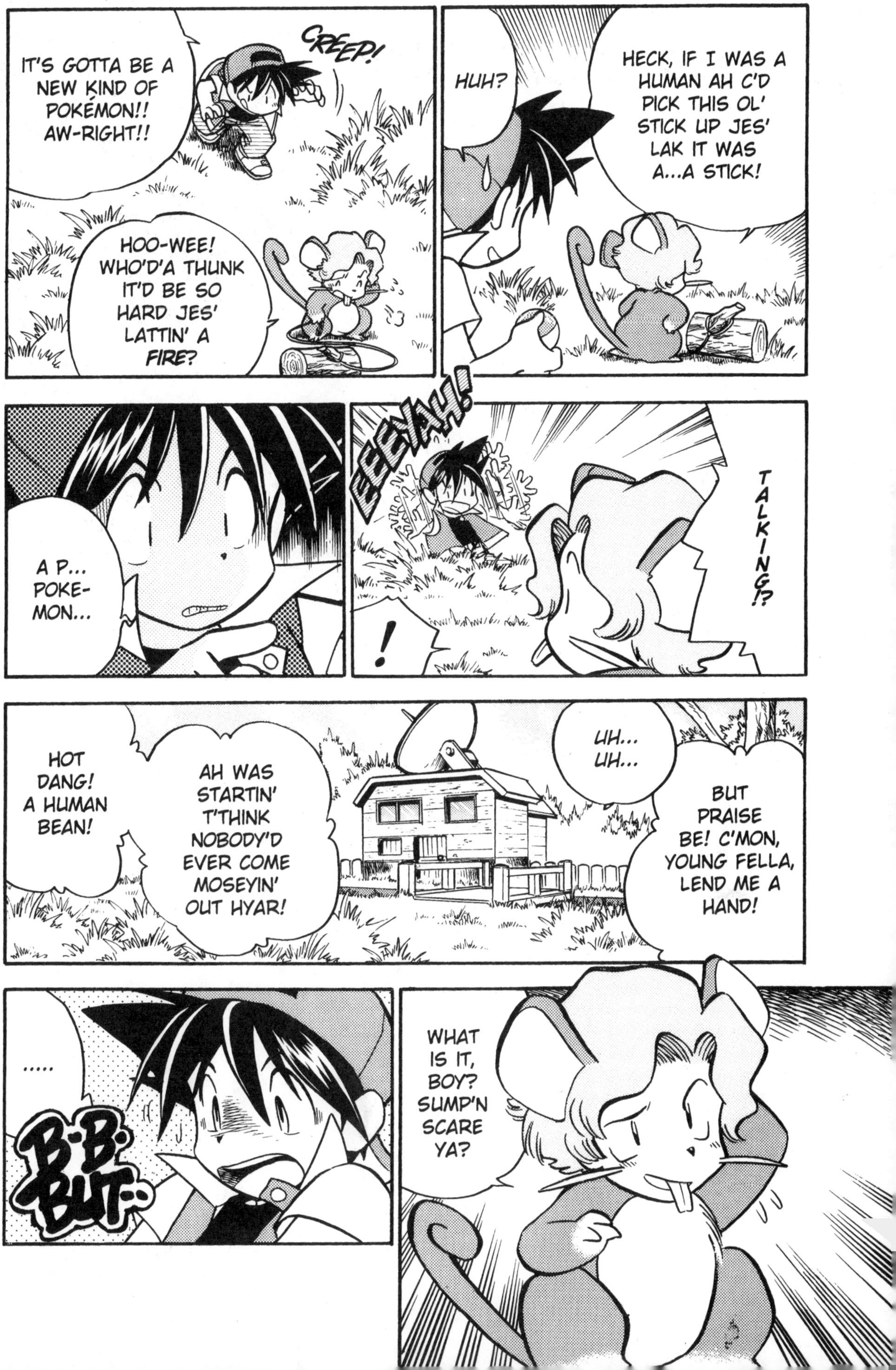
CREEP!
IT'S GOTTA BE A NEW KIND OF POKÉMON!! AW-RIGHT!!
HOO-WEE! WHO'D'A THUNK IT'D BE SO HARD JES' LATTIN' A FIRE?
HUH?
HECK, IF I WAS A HUMAN AH C'D PICK THIS OL' STICK UP JES' LAK IT WAS A...A STICK!
A P... POKE-MON...
EEEYAH!
TALKING!?
!
HOT DANG! A HUMAN BEAN!
AH WAS STARTIN' T'THINK NOBODY'D EVER COME MOSEYIN' OUT HYAR!
UH... UH...
BUT PRAISE BE! C'MON, YOUNG FELLA, LEND ME A HAND!
.....
B-B-BUT...
WHAT IS IT, BOY? SUMP'N SCARE YA?

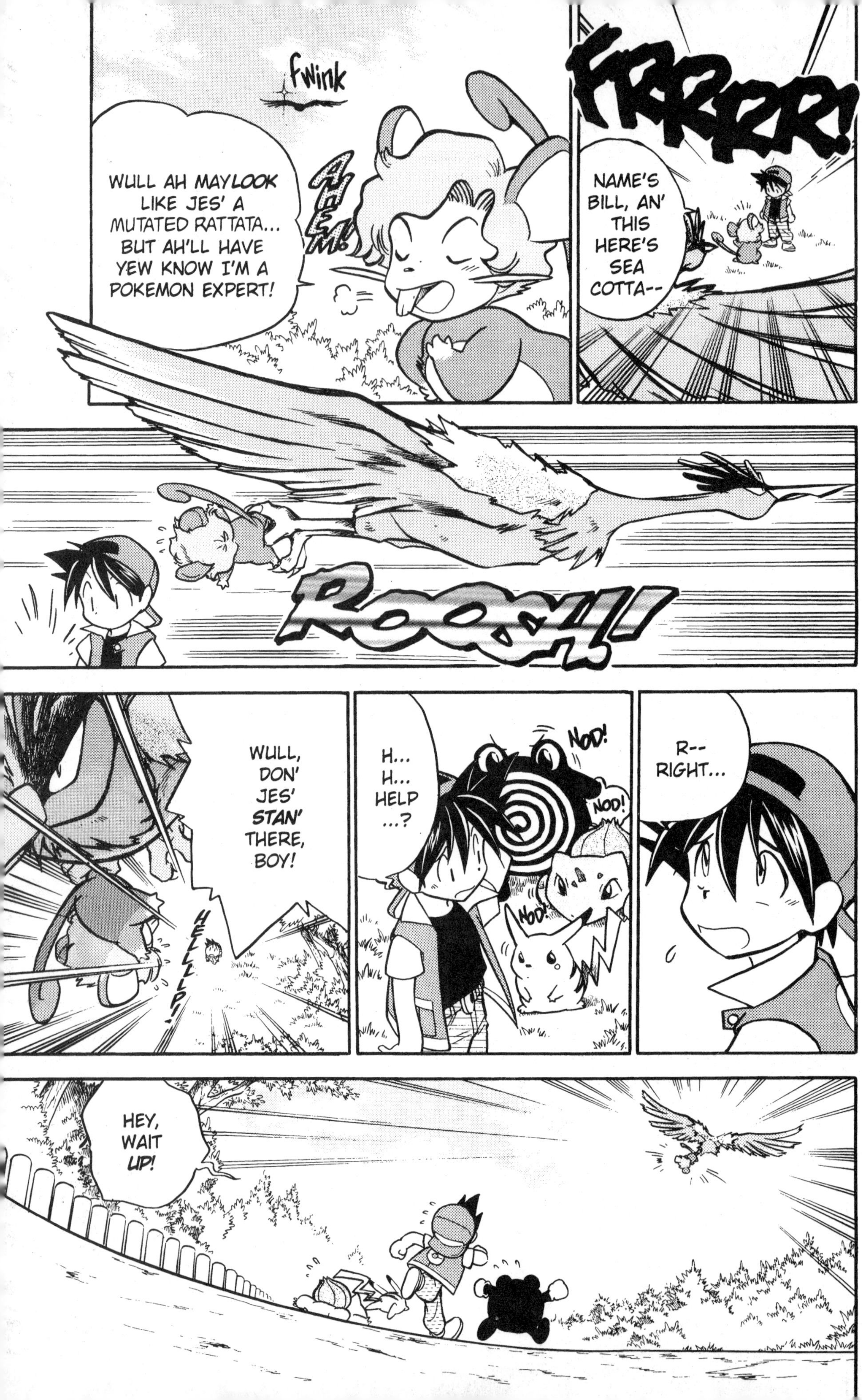
fwink
WULL AH MAY LOOK LIKE JES' A MUTATED RATTATA... BUT AH'LL HAVE YEW KNOW I'M A POKEMON EXPERT!
AHEM!
FRRRR!
NAME'S BILL, AN' THIS HERE'S SEA COTTA--
ROOSH!
WULL, DON' JES' STAN' THERE, BOY!
HELLLP!
H... H... HELP ...?
NOD!
NOD!
NOD!
R-- RIGHT...
HEY, WAIT UP!

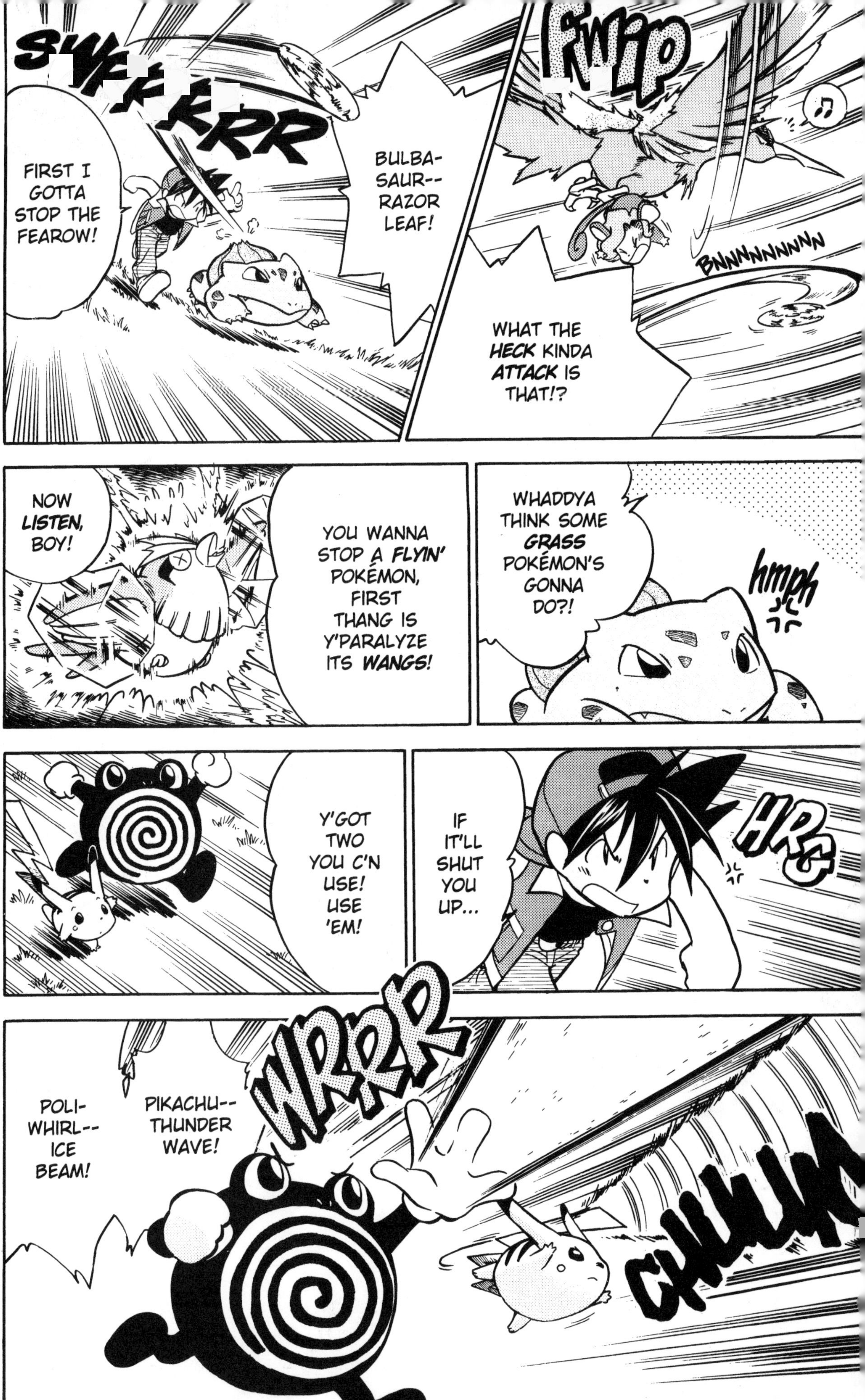
KRRR
FIRST I GOTTA STOP THE FEAROW!
BULBA-SAUR--RAZOR LEAF!
FWIP
BNNNNNNNNN
WHAT THE HECK KINDA ATTACK IS THAT!?
NOW LISTEN, BOY!
YOU WANNA STOP A FLYIN' POKÉMON, FIRST THANG IS Y'PARALYZE ITS WANGS!
WHADDYA THINK SOME GRASS POKÉMON'S GONNA DO?!
hmph
Y'GOT TWO YOU C'N USE! USE 'EM!
IF IT'LL SHUT YOU UP...
HRG
WRRR
POLI-WHIRL--ICE BEAM!
PIKACHU--THUNDER WAVE!

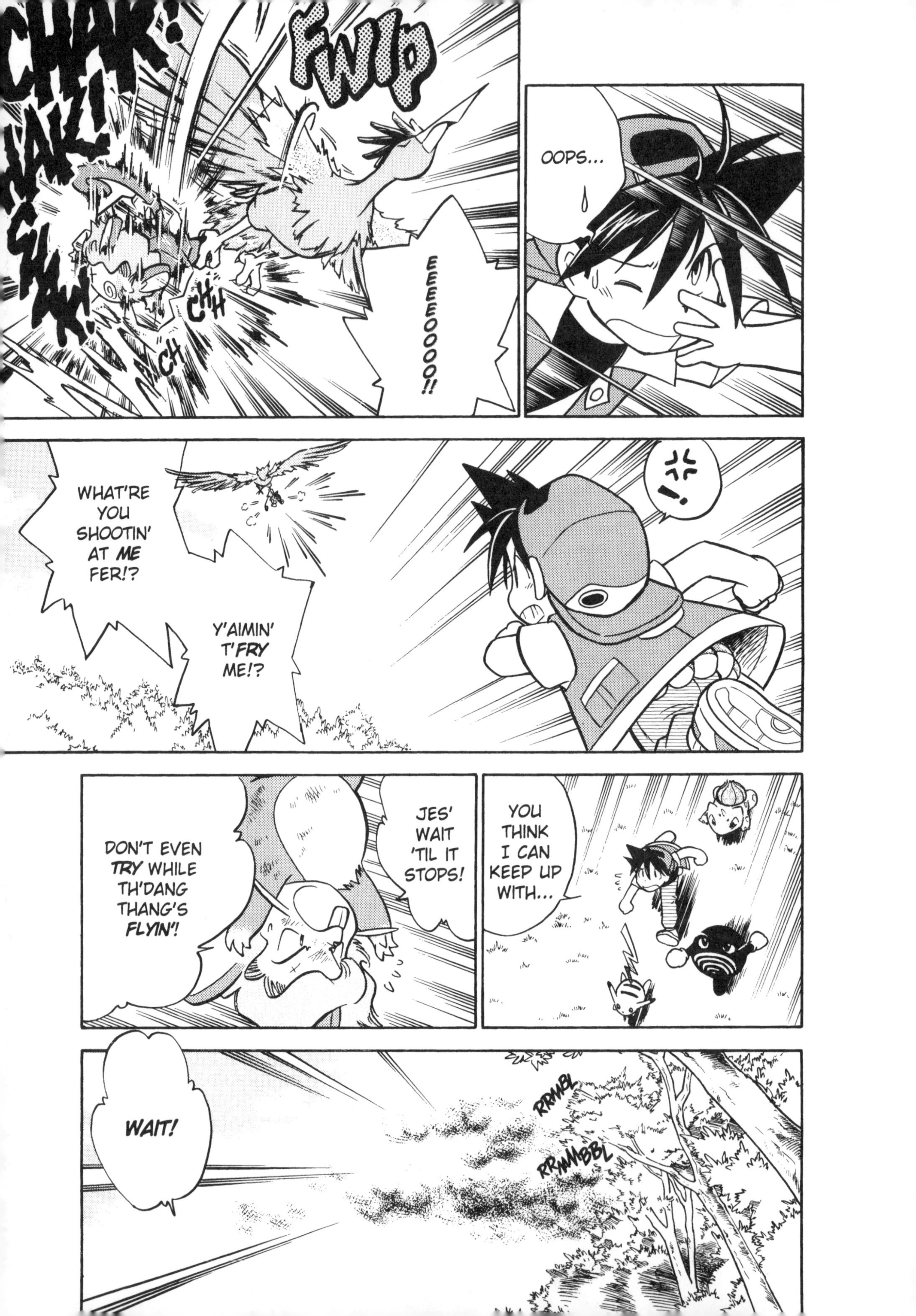
CHAK! HAK! SHAK!
FWIP
CH CH CH
EEEEOOOOO!!
OOPS...
WHAT'RE YOU SHOOTIN' AT ME FER!?
Y'AIMIN' T'FRY ME!?
!
YOU THINK I CAN KEEP UP WITH...
JES' WAIT 'TIL IT STOPS!
DON'T EVEN TRY WHILE TH'DANG THANG'S FLYIN'!
WAIT!
RRMBL
RRAMBBL

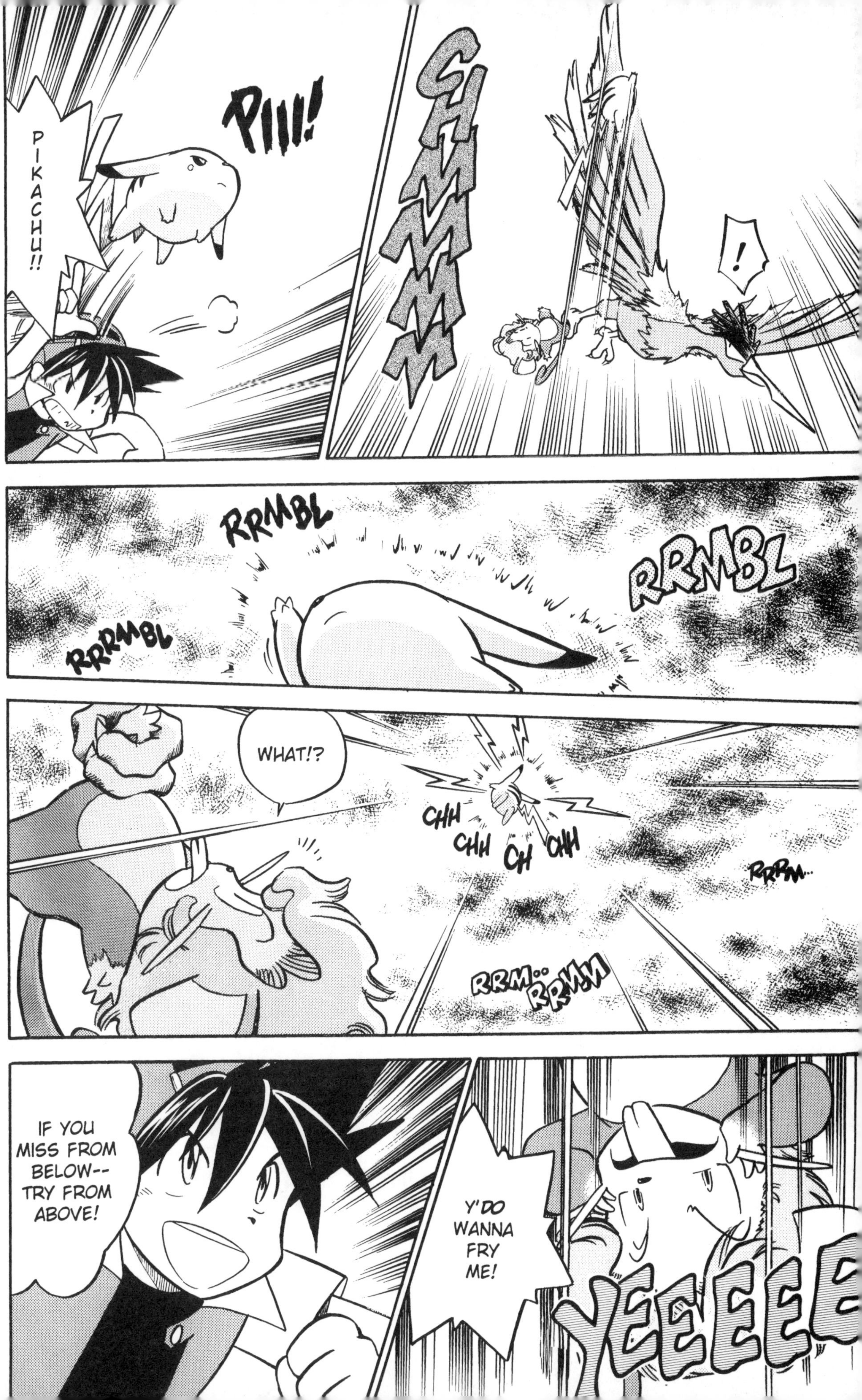
PIKACHU!!
PIII!
CHMMMMM
!
RRMBL
RRMBL
RRRMBL
WHAT!?
CHH
CHH
CH
CHH
RRRM...
RRM.. RRMM
IF YOU MISS FROM BELOW-- TRY FROM ABOVE!
Y'DO WANNA FRY ME!
YEEEEE

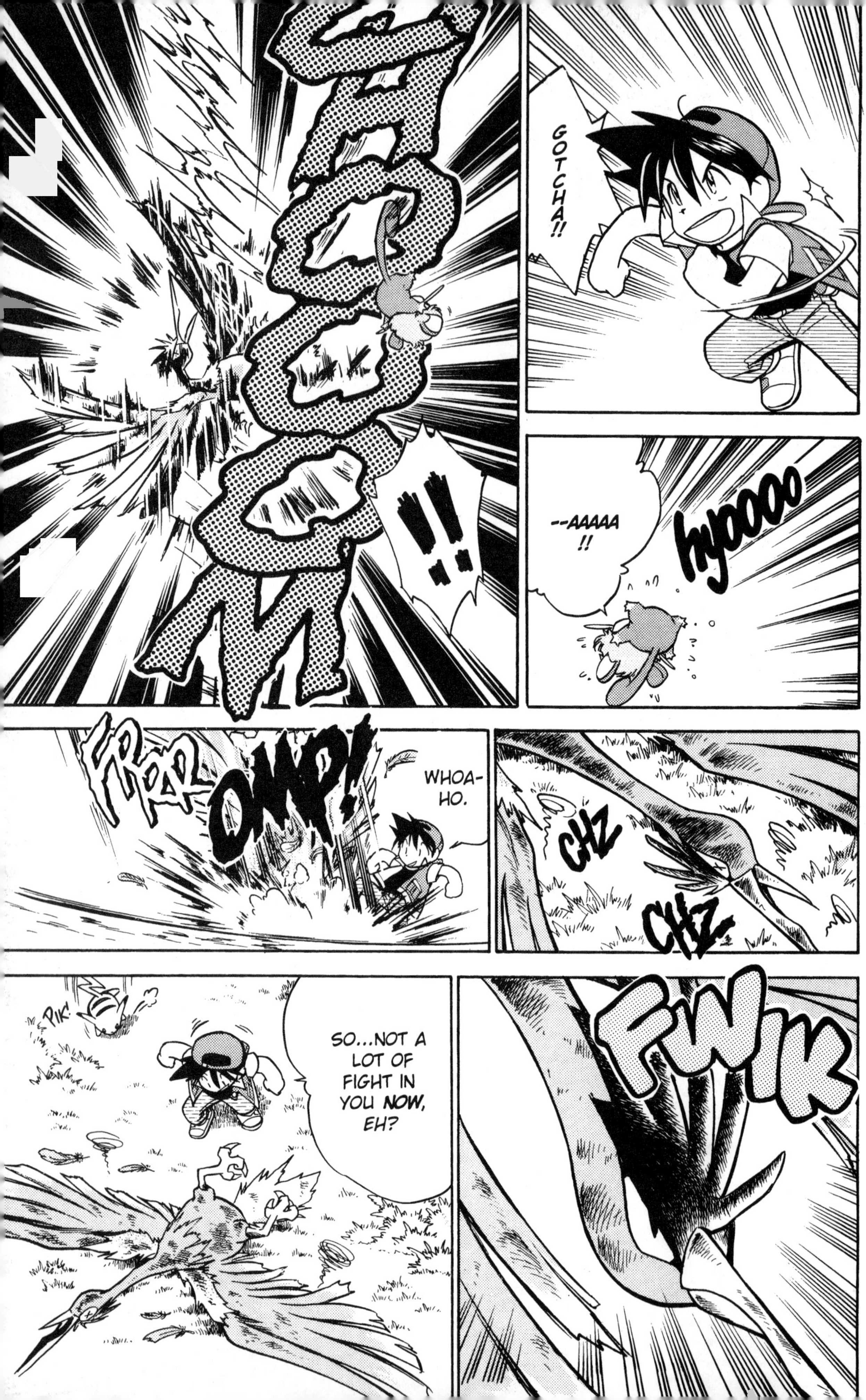
!!
GOTCHA!!
--AAAAA !!
hyoooo
OMP!
WHOA-HO.
CHZ
CHZ
PIK!
SO...NOT A LOT OF FIGHT IN YOU NOW, EH?
FWIK

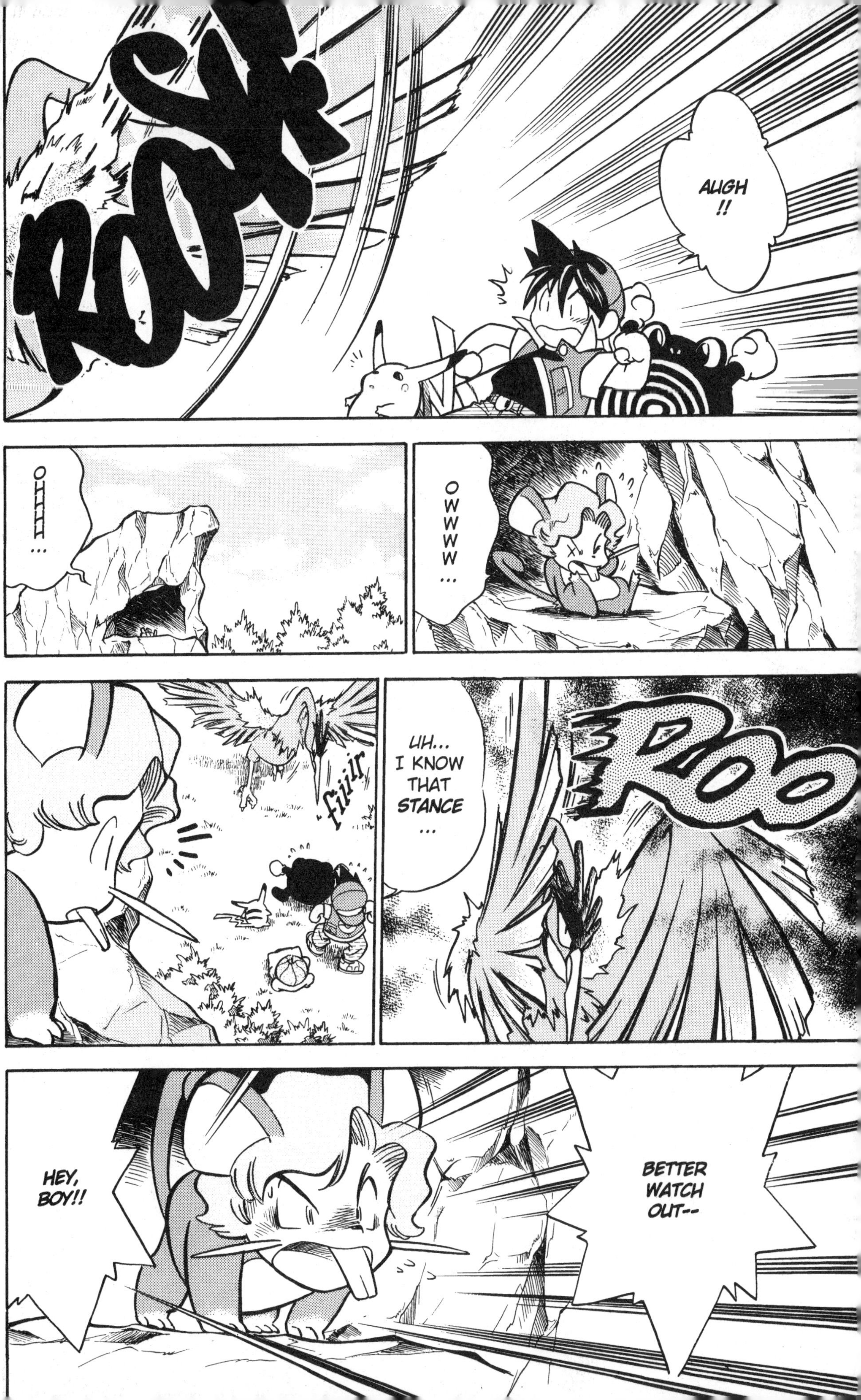
ROOK
AUGH!!
OHHHH...
OWWWW...
fiiiir
UH... I KNOW THAT STANCE...
ROO
HEY, BOY!!
BETTER WATCH OUT--

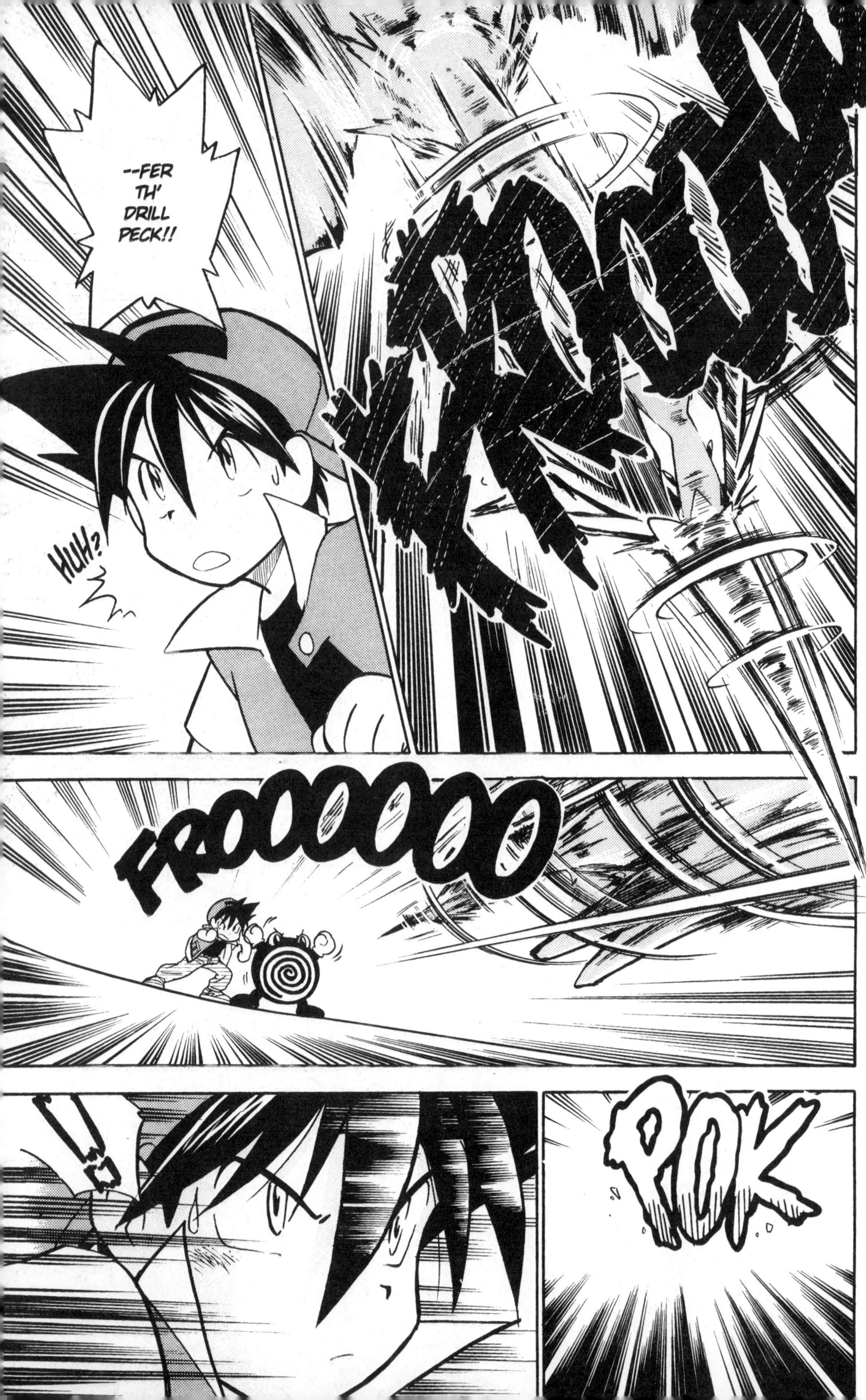
--FER TH' DRILL PECK!!
HUH?
FROOOOOOO
POK

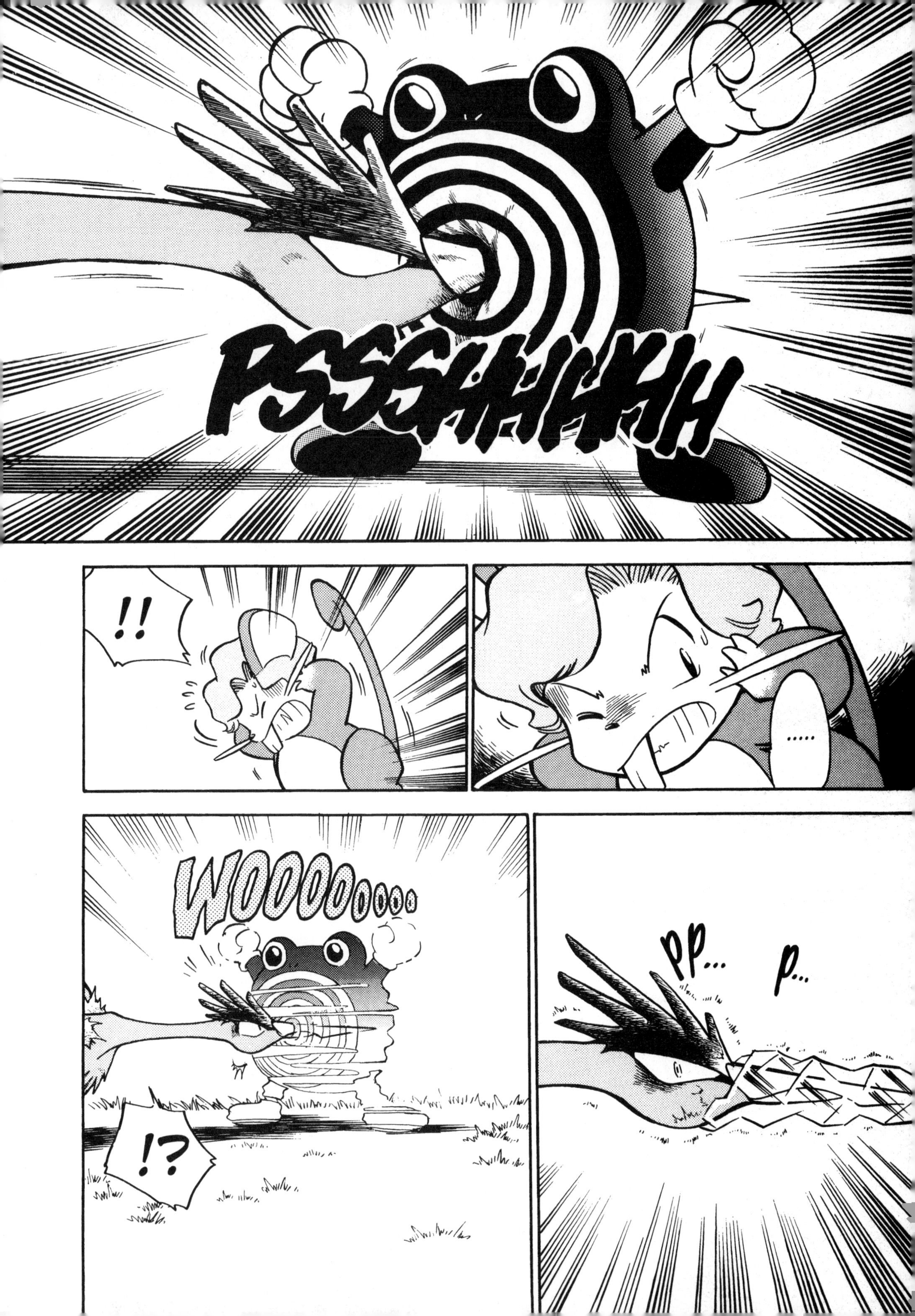
PSSSHHHHH
......
!!
PP... P...
WOOOOOOOO
!?

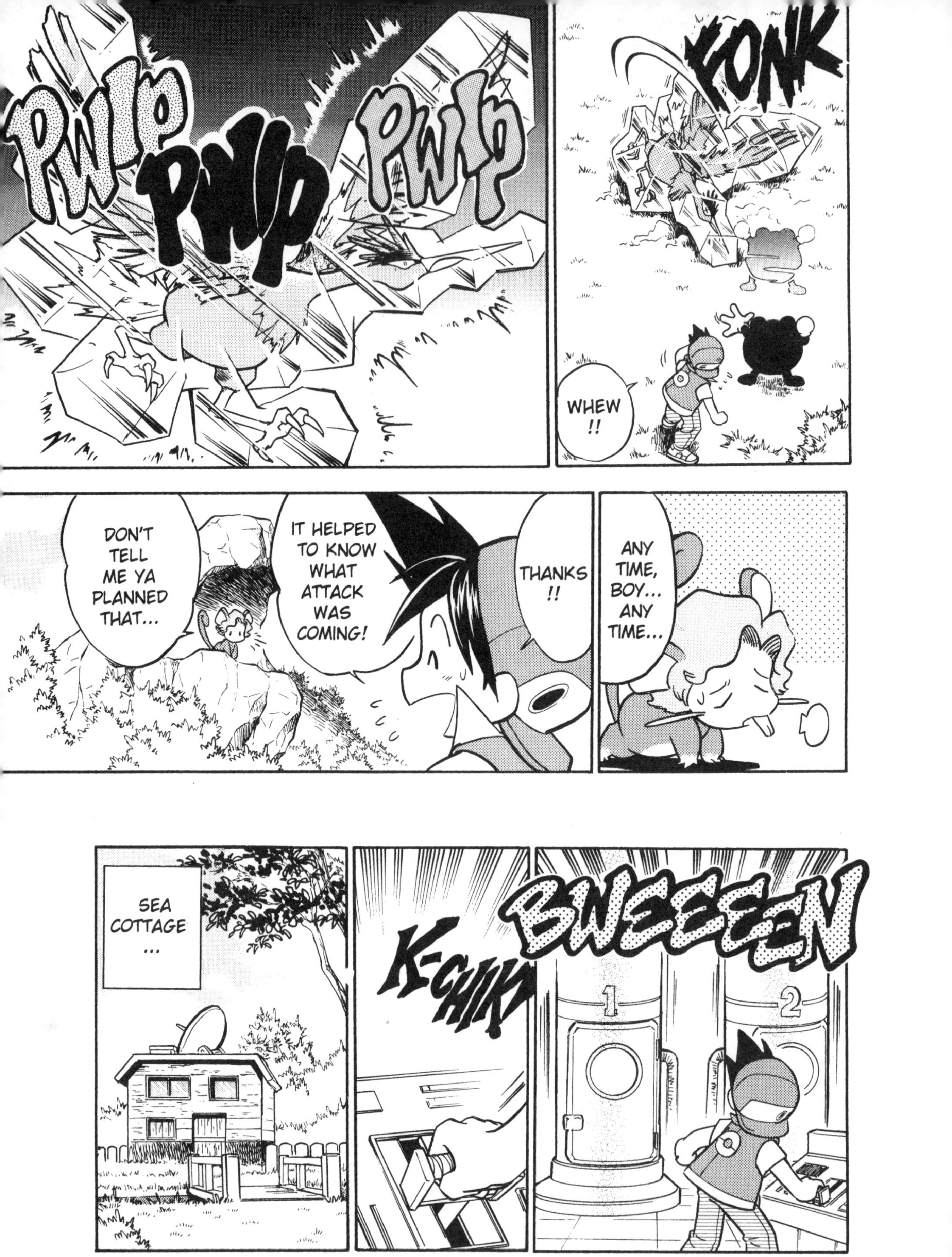
PWIP
PWIP
PWIP
FONK
WHEW !!
DON'T TELL ME YA PLANNED THAT...
IT HELPED TO KNOW WHAT ATTACK WAS COMING!
THANKS !!
ANY TIME, BOY... ANY TIME...
SEA COTTAGE ...
K-CHIK
BWEEEEN

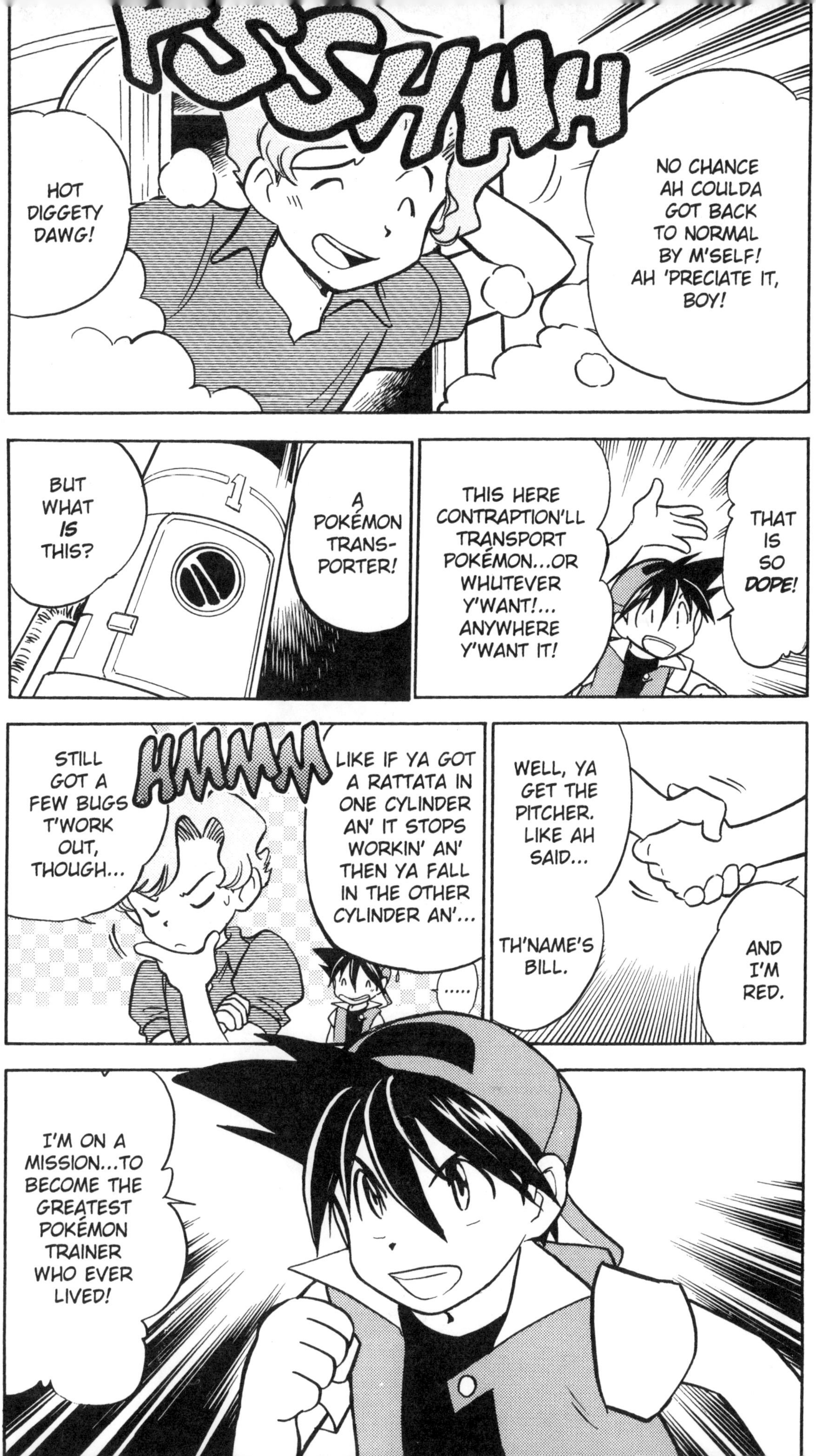
FSSHAH
HOT DIGGETY DAWG!
NO CHANCE AH COULDA GOT BACK TO NORMAL BY M'SELF! AH 'PRECIATE IT, BOY!
BUT WHAT *IS* THIS?
A POKÉMON TRANS-PORTER!
THIS HERE CONTRAPTION'LL TRANSPORT POKÉMON...OR WHUTEVER Y'WANT!... ANYWHERE Y'WANT IT!
THAT IS SO *DOPE!*
HMMM
STILL GOT A FEW BUGS T'WORK OUT, THOUGH...
LIKE IF YA GOT A RATTATA IN ONE CYLINDER AN' IT STOPS WORKIN' AN' THEN YA FALL IN THE OTHER CYLINDER AN'...
.....
WELL, YA GET THE PITCHER. LIKE AH SAID...
TH'NAME'S BILL.
AND I'M RED.
I'M ON A MISSION...TO BECOME THE GREATEST POKÉMON TRAINER WHO EVER LIVED!

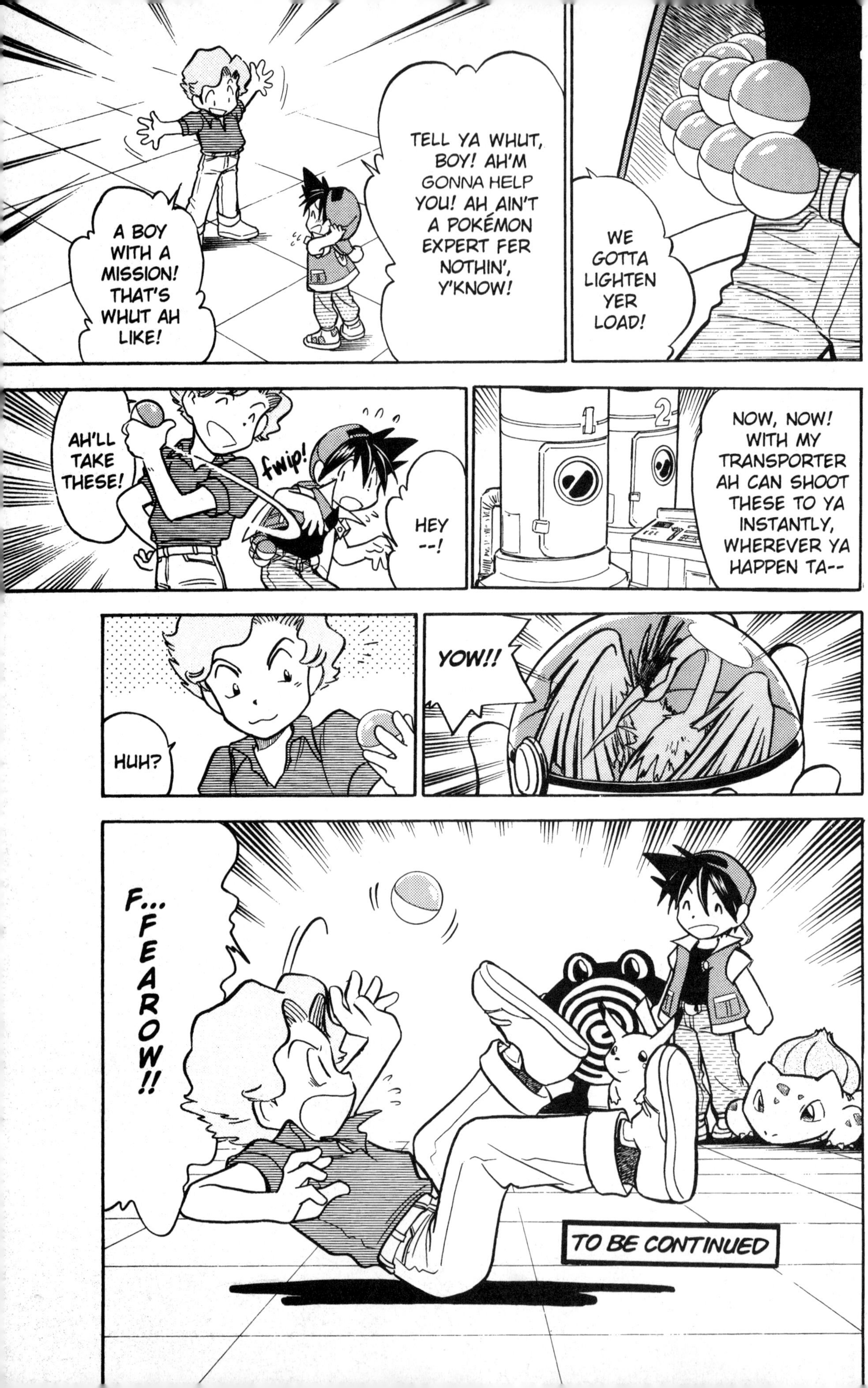
A BOY WITH A MISSION! THAT'S WHUT AH LIKE!
TELL YA WHUT, BOY! AH'M GONNA HELP YOU! AH AIN'T A POKÉMON EXPERT FER NOTHIN', Y'KNOW!
WE GOTTA LIGHTEN YER LOAD!
AH'LL TAKE THESE!
fwip!
HEY --!
NOW, NOW! WITH MY TRANSPORTER AH CAN SHOOT THESE TO YA INSTANTLY, WHEREVER YA HAPPEN TA--
HUH?
YOW!!
F... FEAROW!!
TO BE CONTINUED

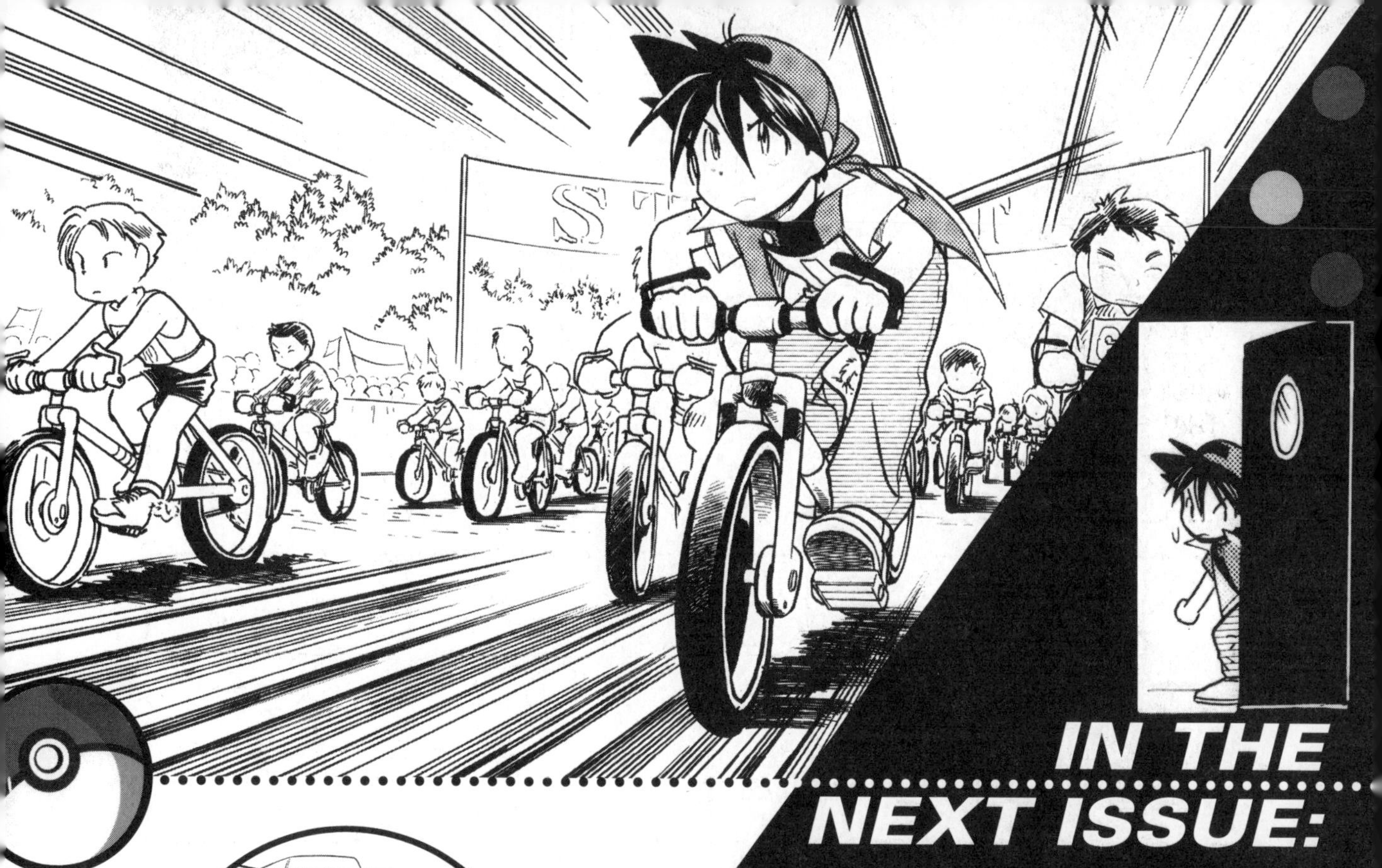

IN THE NEXT ISSUE:

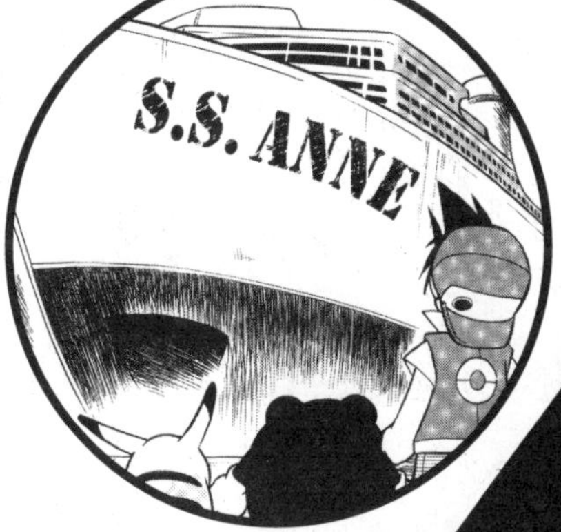
S.S. ANNE

Red has to find out why all the Pokémon in Vermilion City are being stolen!

Shipboard adventures on the S.S. Anne!

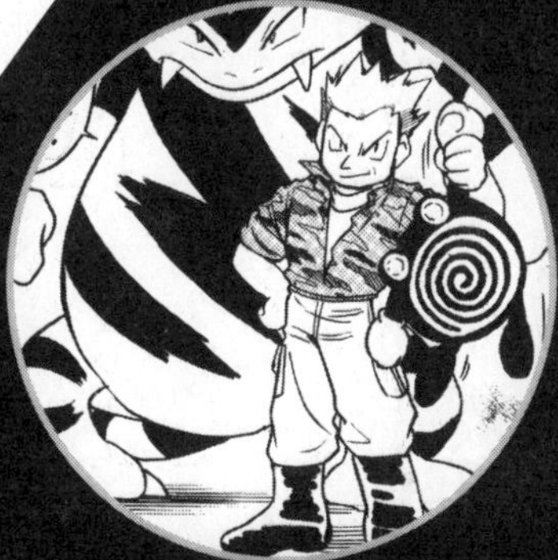

It's Poliwhirl vs. Lt. Surge and Electabuzz!

A bike race through a Pokémon obstacle course!

The biggest, roundest roadblock ever!

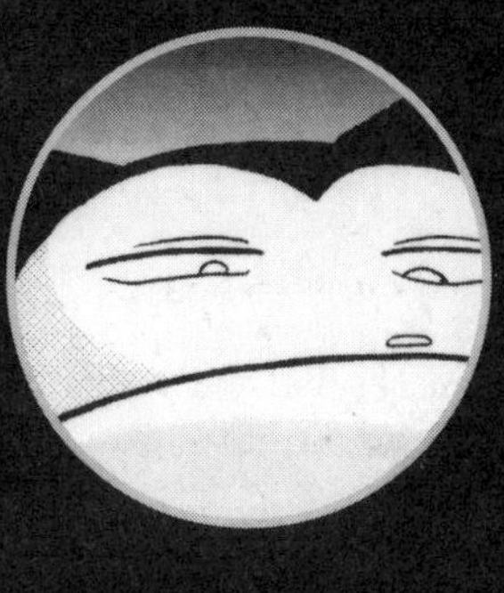

Get the next exciting issue:
SNORLAX STOP
on sale soon!

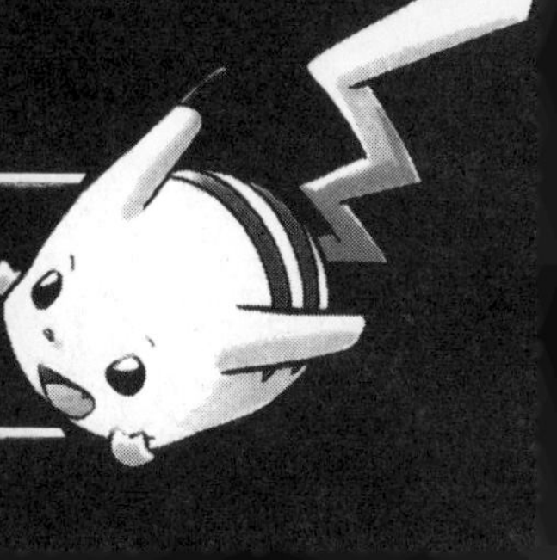

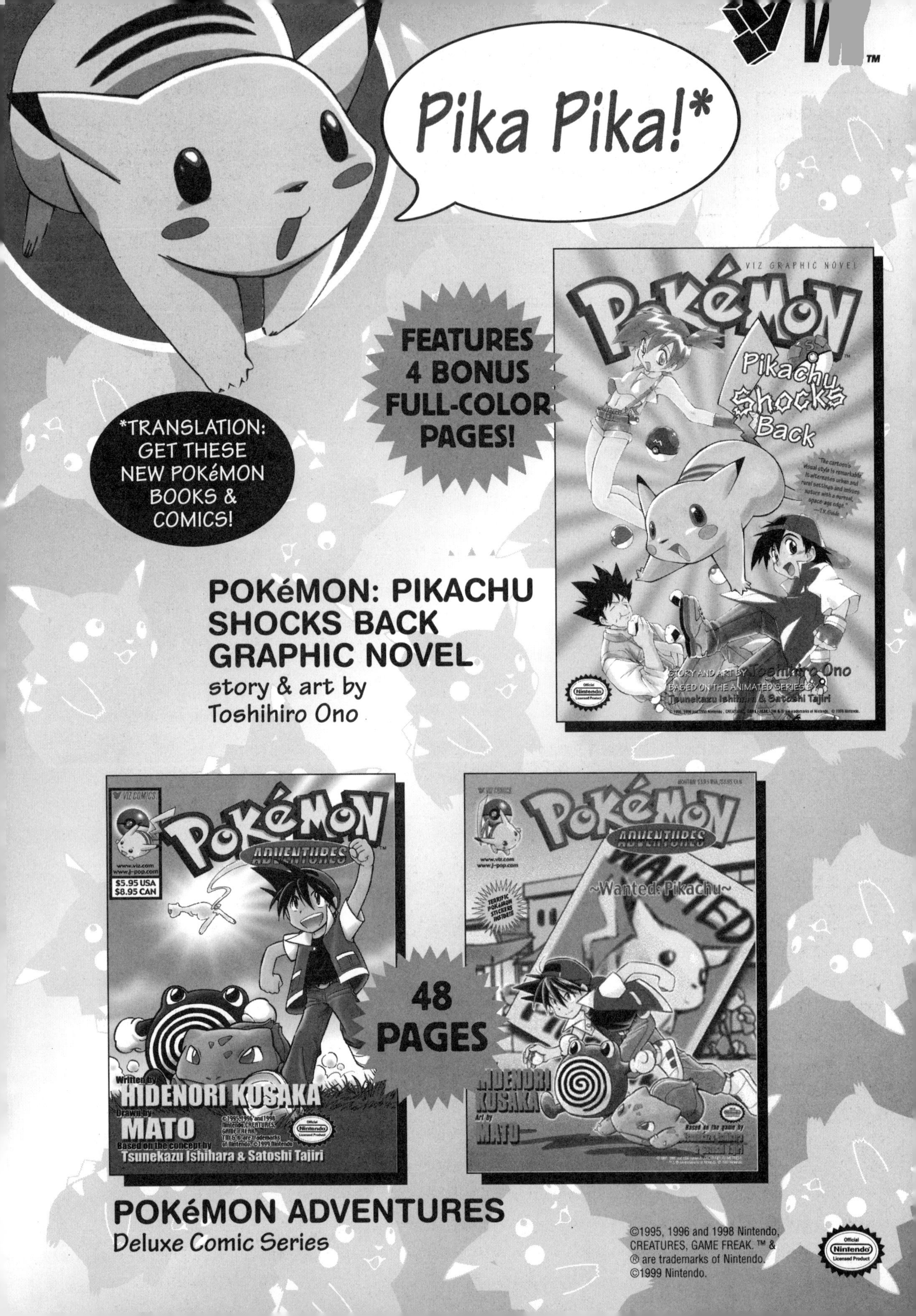

Pika Pika!*
*TRANSLATION: GET THESE NEW POKéMON BOOKS & COMICS!
FEATURES 4 BONUS FULL-COLOR PAGES!
VIZ GRAPHIC NOVEL
POKéMON
Pikachu Shocks Back
POKéMON: PIKACHU SHOCKS BACK GRAPHIC NOVEL
story & art by
Toshihiro Ono
POKéMON ADVENTURES
www.viz.com
www.j-pop.com
$5.95 USA
$8.95 CAN
Written by
HIDENORI KOSAKA
Drawn by
MATO
Based on the concept by
Tsunekazu Ishihara & Satoshi Tajiri
~Wanted: Pikachu~
48 PAGES
POKéMON ADVENTURES
Deluxe Comic Series
©1995, 1996 and 1998 Nintendo, CREATURES, GAME FREAK. ™ & ® are trademarks of Nintendo. ©1999 Nintendo.
Official Nintendo Licensed Product

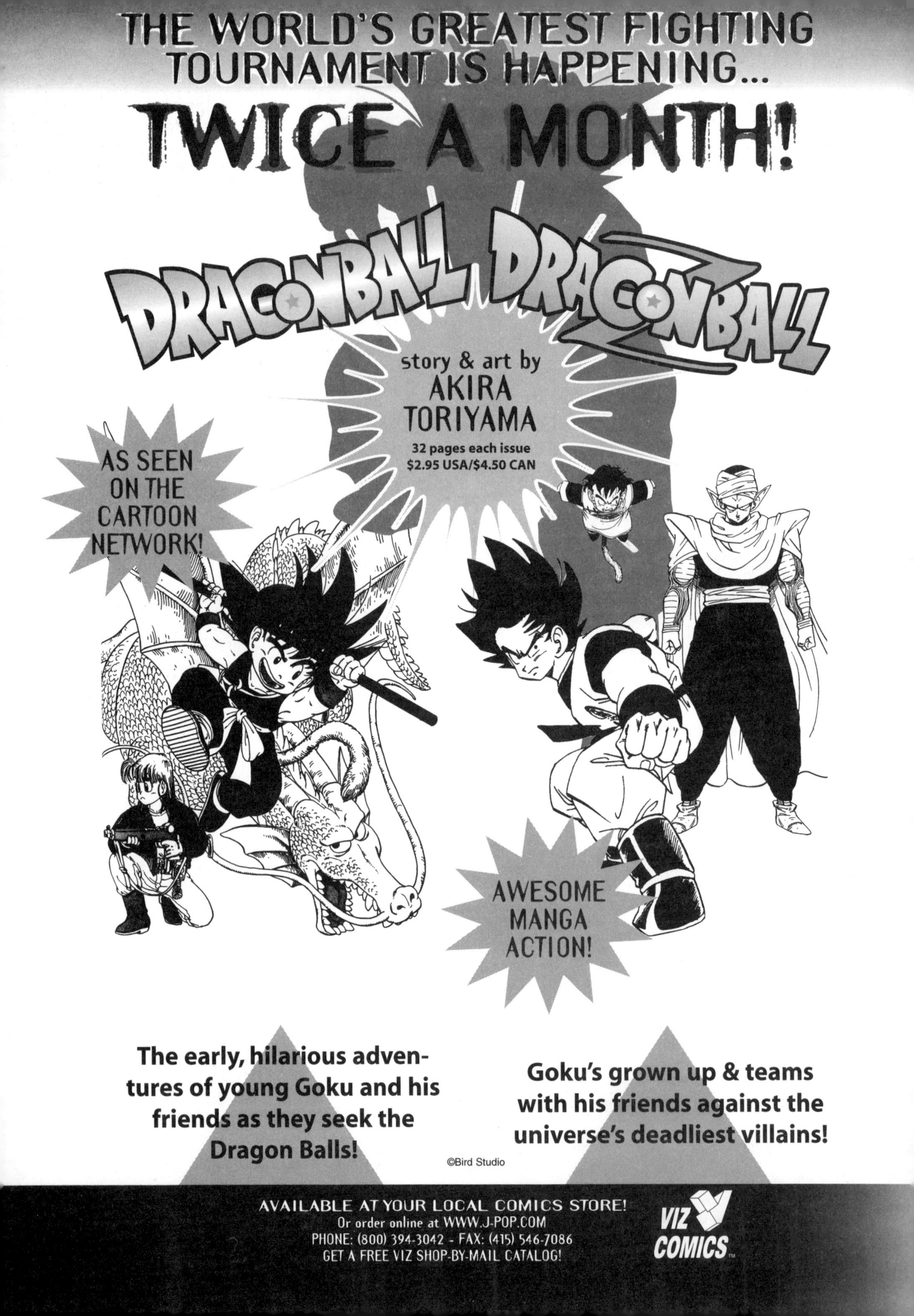
THE WORLD'S GREATEST FIGHTING TOURNAMENT IS HAPPENING...
TWICE A MONTH!
DRAGONBALL
DRAGONBALL Z
story & art by AKIRA TORIYAMA
32 pages each issue
$2.95 USA/$4.50 CAN
AS SEEN ON THE CARTOON NETWORK!
AWESOME MANGA ACTION!
The early, hilarious adventures of young Goku and his friends as they seek the Dragon Balls!
Goku's grown up & teams with his friends against the universe's deadliest villains!
©Bird Studio
AVAILABLE AT YOUR LOCAL COMICS STORE!
Or order online at WWW.J-POP.COM
PHONE: (800) 394-3042 - FAX: (415) 546-7086
GET A FREE VIZ SHOP-BY-MAIL CATALOG!
VIZ COMICS